Industrial Strength Solutions

Build Successful Work Teams!

A Business Life Investment Model

Featuring **The Encounter**
An Experience with
President and Mrs. George W. Bush

Glen Aubrey

www.ctrg.com
www.Leadershipls.com
www.Industrial-Strength-Solutions.com

PublishAmerica
Baltimore

ISBN: 1-4241-1440-3
PUBLISHED BY PUBLISHAMERICA, LLLP
www.publishamerica.com
Baltimore

Printed in the United States of America

Industrial Strength Solutions

Build Successful Work Teams!

A Business Life Investment Model

Featuring **The Encounter**
An Experience with
President and Mrs. George W. Bush

Glen Aubrey

www.ctrg.com
www.Leadershipls.com
www.Industrial-Strength-Solutions.com

Dedication

To the thousands of employers and employees representing incredibly varied fields of endeavor and accomplishment who have taken the principles of *Leadership Is—* and *Industrial Strength Solutions* to heart, head, and hand, and have witnessed these authentic values work with integrity in their multiple work environments, producing positive and enduring results, I dedicate this book.

Permissions and Credits

Contributions of stories and illustrations have come from people who are friends and business associates, two from figures of history and, in the case of the President of the United States, a surprise encounter. I express my sincere appreciation for those granting permission for their stories to be told, or their illustrations to be included. These have enriched the book.

In order of presentation:

Southern Sweet Tea recipe used by permission of Rick and Patti Fleming and Tonya Weddington.

Scripture taken from the *Holy Bible, New International Version*. Copyright 1973, 1978, 1984 International Bible Society. Used by permission of Zondervan Bible Publishers. All rights reserved.

The Combination used with permission of Tom Clark, RPh, MHS.

The CTRG Boxes used with permission of Richard Willis.

The Encounter An experience with President and Mrs. George W. Bush

The Teacher, story of Jack Armstrong, used with permission of his wife, Kathy.

Lincoln letter to J. M. Brockman, Esq. and other Lincoln references are in the public domain.

The Commitment used with permission of Mary Ann Compher.

The Blend used with permission of Larry McNamer.

The Turnabout used with permission of Jo Ann Suarez.

The Learning Experience used with permission of Doug Gadker.

The Balancing Action used with permission of John Gibson.

Word definitions taken from *Merriam-Webster's 11th Collegiate Dictionary*. Copyright 2003, Merriam-Webster, Incorporated.

"If" by Rudyard Kipling is in the public domain.

Table of Contents

Before

Several years ago I learned a distinct difference between sweetened iced tea and Southern sweet tea, and I learned this distinction both by description and taste. Speaking to a group in Tennessee for a series of meetings spanning a week, I was captivated with how I was received (coming from Southern California, they may not have known what to expect!), and discovered soon upon arrival that I was intentionally placed in an honored position of receiving abundant doses of warm Southern hospitality, including mountains of delectable food, great conversation, contagious laughter, family closeness, and tea—lots and lots of tea, essentially two kinds from which to choose, regular iced tea, and sweet tea. And the differences between those two are noticeable indeed.

In Southern California, where we reside, we can select from many varieties of tea including iced, of course, herbal (a big favorite of many in this State, especially near the beaches), oriental teas, caffeine and non-caffeine types and many more. But only in the South did my taste buds relish their first acquaintance with sweet tea, and very nearly only in the South has my desire for enjoying more sweet tea become satisfied in remembrance of that first sip. That satisfaction is only achieved with what has to be the genuine article, and I'm writing to tell you, that genuine article tastes mighty fine. Understand here that the method of making tea sweet where I live is by adding sugar — at times mountains of it — to tea already poured over ice. In Tennessee, Georgia, Florida, and I am told throughout the South, sweet tea is the result of combining necessary ingredients as part of the actual process of making the tea, not the product of an addition after the fact. Bottom line, sweet tea simply tastes better. *Its character is inherent in its make-up.*

I know I could have used flavored coffee vs. coffee flavoring for the illustration, and for those of us who prefer coffee over tea (I would be one of those, especially in the morning) the point is the same, and it is simply this: building great work teams in any business environment has more to do not with combinations of people who may or may not produce well together because we try to combine right elements, including personalities, education, competence and skill sets. Rather, success for great and effective teams is more assuredly founded, and dependent on, people's characters, their core essence traits, their internal compositions, which, when mixed together, yield strong and enduring commitments based on core values agreement, and the cooperation of their networks and interconnectivities, competencies and desires.

When people are combined on work teams on the basis of agreements of essence and essential core values, their work environments become places where their talents and abilities reflect heart-felt longings for excellence in contribution that demonstrate proper alignments of people and production, proving this unalterable premise: people are more important than the products they produce.

Fostering a work environment where people who share like values and dedication build one another first and provision product second is the responsibility of the leader who sees people as vitally important in their persons as primary over their functional expertise. The leader who sets basic parameters of "Relationships precede and give definition to function" because "People are more important than what they do" is the leader who is growing great people who produce better products—in that order. The thread that intertwines the leader's desires with the followers' contributions is the declared and shared truth of the inherent importance of the folks who do the functions, and the agreement within that truth that the process of development is more important than the end deliverable; that, in fact, the process is one of the most significant deliverables in and of itself.

Where people-importance is primary, production with excellence is manifested in multiple and recurring day-to-day work place experiences: as communication loops are closed, all-important large and small details are attended to, right attitudes birth right actions, goals are fulfilled ahead of time and above expectation, budgets are adhered to, humility characterizes working atmospheres, and support of individuals on the team replaces tired, ineffectual and often fruitless efforts, wasted energy, and low morale—traits that so often accompany, and are descriptive of, so many contemporary work environments. These lines of demarcation between valued and devalued people and processes are not hard to recognize where both exist. The encouraging truth is that any environment can be changed at any time by any people who truly desire growth in their work place and who want to produce better environments and heightened excellence in their product.

Any environment can be changed at any time by any people who truly desire growth in their work place and who want to produce better environments and heightened excellence in their product.

There are many choices as to what kinds of teams an organization wants to build, and what that organization should expect to contribute to these teams and receive from them. The processes of choosing what kinds of teams are desired involve numerous considerations, of course, but the bottom line is to be found in this question and the answer to it, whether one is a follower or a leader: Do you want to help create and involve yourself in the workings of a team where people are treated as valuable and therefore produce value-added contributions, or do you want to be satisfied with work groups as usual where production is too often consumptive of the people who produce it? The answer to that question will give meaning to the assimilation of the context and content, the principles and practices described in *Industrial Strength Solutions.*

If you are serious about learning and growth, the mix of what you read and how you incorporate the elements of truth into your life and work experience will tell you beyond doubt whether the principles you see on the page are the principles you choose to engage, that if applied can become the verifiable evidence of the good choices you make in daily work life. These choices become the traits other people see and wish to duplicate because of who you are in your character and who you choose to become at your core.

> Do you want to help create and involve yourself in the workings of a team where people are treated as valuable and therefore produce value-added contributions, or do you want to be satisfied with work groups as usual where production is too often consumptive of the people who produce it?

It's a lot like making sweet tea as opposed to making tea sweet. As an illustration, I took the liberty of checking with Rick, simply one of my best friends, a good ol' Tennessee boy (once a Californian, since removed to the South), and his very dear wife, Patti, along with one of Rick's co-workers, Tonya, to ascertain the process of making Southern Sweet Tea. In this method the sweetness is "organic" to the mixture as opposed to becoming the result of sugar added to an existing liquid after the production is finished.

The tea recipe below, according to Patti, was "served many years at Grandma's table, mama's table, and mine." Without a whole lot of fanfare, but with a sure desire for a better result in mind from the outset, here is how it's done.

Southern Sweet Tea

"Well, first you get a 2 qt. sauce pan and fill it ¾ full of water, place on high heat, and bring to a boil. If you're using family size tea bags, use 3, if you're using small bags, use 8. Tie tea bags together by their strings. Remove tags. While the water is heating, put tea bags in the water. When it boils, cover and remove from heat. Steep 30 minutes. Get a 2 qt. jug and add 1½ cups of sugar, more or less to your liking. (Please note: a true Southerner does not use sugar substitute in their tea.) Pour hot tea over sugar leaving tea bags in pot. Fill pot with water (making sure water pours over tea bags to get all the flavor) and add to jug until full. Stir until sugar is completely dissolved. Refrigerate until ready to serve. Place tea in glass pitcher and float thinly sliced lemons on top. Now the best part: Get you a glass (not a plastic tumbler), fill it with ice, and pour the tea over the ice. Add a sprig of mint or a slice of lemon. Then go set in the recliner, put your feet up, relax, and enjoy! Southern Sweet Tea is best when shared with a friend on a lazy afternoon."

The key here is "Pour hot tea over sugar…." The character of the process of composition creates the integrity of the final product. Much in the same way, great teams in the work place are formed and function. The essentials of character are not compromised as these people are brought together; rather, characters are blended in unity upon first-priority agreements of a strong value system, dedicated from the outset that because they value each other and are committed to each other's success, they will contribute that of which they are able of their own strengths to assure excellence, creating and growing a workable solution of tremendous force and resiliency, and a model that endures.

During 1862, at a height of profound discouragement for the Union in America's Civil War, President Abraham Lincoln was faced with the awesome consideration of weighing mounting and incredible costs of lives sacrificed and property decimated on both sides. The results he and the country endured appeared at that time to be far from justified or satisfactory; indeed, they were at many moments monumentally discouraging beyond words. A victory for the Union seemed distant at best. It was during these forlorn and lonely seasons for the president, as defeat upon defeat converged from multiple sources, that Lincoln made insurmountably tough decisions. He had to. His choices would make or break not only the conduct of the war, but ultimately determine the Union's success or failure. Criticism from within and conflict from without made his process of decision-making harder yet, but true greatness shone and he chose what he deemed best.

Upon his resolve to continue to move down the path he had selected, because he believed and declared he was acting as an instrument of the people to uphold the Constitution and save the Union, he enacted a war and humanitarian measure that forever put the blight of slavery on its path of eventual destruction. That measure was, of course, the Emancipation Proclamation. The Union armies could benefit from the manpower the emancipated slaves would provide, and the slaves that were freed were those who at that time were located in the States that had rebelled. Not ever referring to the Confederacy as a separate country, only as States "then in rebellion" to the United States, he exercised his authority over and on behalf of the people held as slaves within those States, who, because of their freedom, helped the Union win the war and preserve the country from disastrous dissolution.

When Lincoln was assassinated it was said that the South lost one of its greatest supporters, and it was true, for as part of the plan to restore the Union, in addition to the Emancipation Proclamation, Lincoln had articulated in the weeks and days just before his death his desires to make the process of restoration and reconstruction as right and accessible for achievement as possible. To empower the States that had rebelled to rejoin the Union, Lincoln was not in favor of burdening them with unnecessary measures born of a spirit of vindictiveness or punitive subjugation; rather, he asked only for fundamental requirements needed as basis points to unify the country in the short term and reinstate the States for a United States that would endure in perpetuity.

As he closed his Second Inaugural address, delivered on March 4, 1865, he proclaimed these words, "With malice toward none; with charity for all; with firmness in the right, as God gives us to see the right, let us strive on to finish the work we are in; to bind up the nation's wounds; to care for him who shall have borne the battle, and for his widow, and his orphan—to do all which may achieve and cherish a just and lasting peace among ourselves, and with all nations." These immortal words were addressed to a country that despaired of war and was desperate for peace, and they came at the time when Appomattox was still weeks away, but it was coming, and eventually did.

Some truths are worth believing, desiring, risking for, and acting upon. The union of the United States of America was certainly one of them. The union, or perhaps better put, the unification coming from essential agreement on values, goals, people, process and product may be representative of other more contemporary causes. These considerations, while not requiring the extent of a sacrifice of civil war, may inspire courage and boldness based on right attitudes and attributes that will encourage people who agree to engage in right actions to produce better results than the status quo, especially if the status quo is not producing well, or if people on teams in your organization are involved in their own uncivil wars.

Consider and weigh your work environment against what

you might like it to be if it could be shown that through your contributions, stemming from your true desire for improvement to be accomplished in best methods, it could become markedly better. In what ways could the cooperation between workers be strengthened, problems solved, communication improved, trust more genuinely granted and evidenced, customers served with more accuracy and timeliness, and additional profit realized from the combination of these elements mixing together well? And what role, if any, would *you* like to play in initiating action to bring about better results?

The workable solutions that Lincoln proposed, produced, and dedicated himself to completing were founded on solid and essential truths from which he would not waver, regardless of cost, criticism, political sacrifices, and immense tolls that weighed upon him and his family, not to mention the thousands of families forever scarred by the awful effects of battles and immense personal losses, where, bereft of sustenance and means of supply, people in both the North and the South suffered long, some never recovering. An agenda that endures in any environment will be one established on lasting principles that constitute an unshakable mix—a combination of values, desires and actions that are destined to produce good and right results if followed through, because the engagement is proven to be the proper course of action, and the people are wholly dedicated to its process and prospect, regardless of the cost.

It is this kind of industrial strength solution-provision and authenticity of character that current commerce craves. In a market environment where needs for deeds based on core values is growing, this authenticity is demanded from and created by the people who do the work, regardless of their positions, if they want it earnestly enough.

Those who know that business effectiveness is not just determined by the bottom line understand, of course, that hard work is needed, and they are willing to expend dedicated energy required to achieve the results an industry requires, but these results are shown not only in profit margins; instead, they are first demonstrated in improved processes that build frameworks for success, treat people as valuable, building those who within themselves and in cooperation with each other provide the strength of industry to produce the great solutions. These people and their teams, along with their contributions, can be deemed truly "value-added." The commerce world, in which we engage, longs for these additions. For those with a view toward building people and production—in that order—these additions are not optional; they are the essential elements in what may be to some a brand new mixture of solution provision in organizations where people produce because they want to, as opposed to being pushed to achieve provision because they have to.

If this sounds too good to be true, take heart, it isn't. In fact, it's good only because it is true. The willful engagement of principled truth in the real life work place's daily grinds represents some of the most difficult efforts ever expended to accomplish best goals, including required deliverables. Creating, maintaining, developing, and expanding industrial strength solutions that are applicable because they are reliable do not rest on theory. They stand on proven demonstration because principles endure whenever they're applied with integrity. Since the principles are true then it must follow that they will work in every environment eventually, if given the opportunity of real work and life engagement.

Industrial Strength Solutions is described in its sub-title as "A Business Life Investment Model." Simply, this means that once constructed, the model becomes a vital and living standard that can and indeed must be duplicated and expanded in manifold applications. In cooperation with the principles articulated in *Leadership Is—* (www.LeadershipIs.com), this book serves as a natural extension of enduring and true-to-life representations of instilled principles that help leaders and teams win repeatedly. A team that consistently incorporates lasting values and principles into daily practice regimens lives and contributes within its durability and passes along its model to those who seek to follow.

Industrial Strength Solutions is a book about your work place, the way it is, and the way you may want it to be in form and function. Its contents will focus on methods you can use in building successful work teams. The study describes environments formed through preferred, and less-than-desirable mixes of people, in chapters titled, "Office Chemistry 101A," "Winning vs. Whining," "Nitpicking and Petty Criticism," and "Mixing and Matching—Work the Workable Solutions." Stability factors within teams of people who work well form focus topics in chapters titled, "Compliment Your Complement," "Strength Is a Condition—But It Is Not Conditional," and "Attributes of Industrial Strength Solutions." Finally, placing people first and focusing on their desires are positioned in chapters titled, "Achieving Balance," "Come, Work Where I Do: Creating Industrial Strength Solutions in Your Organization," and "Building a Productive Work Environment." "Before" and "After" sections prepare and review, encouraging readers to consider behavioral change. "Permissions and Credits," information about Creative Team Resources Group, Inc. (CTRG: www.ctrg.com) along with selected CTRG tools, "Final Thoughts and Reinforcement," and "Acknowledgments" provide bookends, front and back.

Throughout the book real-life work place stories or interviews are provided as illustrations and proof points. All of the stories are true. In most of these the names of the people involved are not changed and are used with their explicit permissions. Also included are true stories that beg to be told because they are vital to the dissemination of facts and features they so graphically illustrate. In these instances associated names and industries are changed. The names of participants and business enterprises or companies contained in these illustrations are purely fictitious; any resemblance within these stories to any existing company, or to names of any individuals that correspond to, or match those within the stories, is purely coincidental.

"Mix it up," as it is said. That phrase can mean, among many options, the opening of a boxing match, the stirring of a batch of cookie dough, or the process of making sweet tea. It can also mean something significant for you unrelated to boxing, cookies, or tea. You may wish to make the phrase signify your desire to become part of a solution provision that apart from your involvement would simply be incomplete and less effective. With your affirmative decision, however, you can take your place as one who participates fully, born of your earnest desires to create strength in your organization as a living business investment model for others to see and emulate.

> An agenda that endures in any environment will be one established on lasting principles that constitute an unshakable mix—a combination of values, desires and actions that are destined to produce good and right results if followed through, because the engagement is proven to be the proper course of action, and the people are wholly dedicated to its process and prospect, regardless of the cost.

Will you engage and become an ingredient in the creation of success mixtures on your team? Let's see.

Chapter 1:
Office Chemistry 101A

Remember High School Chemistry? How did you do in that class? It may have been awhile, and you may have not considered this formula recently, but what happens when you mix vinegar and soda?

Well, don't run to your kitchen to try it just yet—let's explain it first.

Wisdom literature, Proverbs 25:20, says this: "Like one who takes away a garment on a cold day, or like vinegar poured on soda, is one who sings songs to a heavy heart." (NIV)

It doesn't feel good, it's inappropriate, and it's volatile.

The Combination

Tom Clark, RPh, MHS is a good friend, and absolutely my "Favorite Pharmacist." In talking with him about the intent of this chapter, here is what he reminded me: The mixture of acetic acid CH_3COOH (vinegar) in combination with sodium bicarbonate $NaHCO_3$ (baking soda), creates CO_2 (carbon dioxide gas) and that mixture can propel a rocket. In a work environment it generally makes havoc if these chemicals represent opposing personalities. Consider: If your workplace was a "lab" for mixing and matching people who by their presence and contributions formed the elements for manufacturing a workable solution, who's the vinegar? What kind of attitude and atmosphere accompanied his or her arrival to work today? Who's the baking soda? Have these two intermingled, and if so, has the work day chaos begun?

Explosive components in personalities are often given as features as to why people can't work together. "Don't combine them," you're warned. "Your office, too, can erupt." Keep them apart, on separate teams, in divided cubicles, working on different projects, and all may yet be well.

Alternatively, iron becomes stronger when combined with manganese—in fact when they are combined they produce a metal far stronger than when they are on their own. Throw in a little carbon to the combination, and you can "steel" the moment. Put together the right personalities and then you've got success.

These chemical illustrations proclaim that the leader's job may be to combine strengths and avoid weaknesses for the people he or she oversees, because the leader is responsible, on top of everything else, to create distinct groupings on the basis of workable personalities out of which heightened production comes. The leader searches high and low for combos that work, and then unites them to make better production possible. Right?

Wrong. The leader has many jobs, but this is certainly not one of them.

Ask yourself: what's the chemistry of the compounded individuals that make up your workplace? How do the chemical groupings of the personalities represented in your work environment laboratory fit into the molds of science, or do they fit at all? How much time, if you are the leader, do you spend trying to put people together because you think that certain personality types in specific blends have got to make the positive differences? Sure, these processes work sometimes, many do; but the effort required treats symptoms, not causes.

And the results will not be consistent over the long haul, countermanding what science demands: repeatable proofs.

Here's why: human behaviors, the study of which certainly is a science, are not scientifically determined beyond doubt. What is demonstrated to be true more often than not is that behaviors are driven by character and decision. Behaviors may seek to rule but they are also subject to rules. Behaviors alter the composition of the atmospheres around them. Behaviors cause personalities to submit to them, as behaviors are subject to the decisions of their owners. Behaviors change, and should. People are the change agents, and values are the reasons why conduct is subject to modification. Behaviors are choices.

Since we are considering exploding things, let's blow the chemical theory to kingdom come. None of the above applies to the office environment where human beings choose to create industrial solutions and solutions within industry that work. If you are the leader you are aware of this: too often personality differences morph into multiple and unending excuses employed to cover gross lack of function, plain selfishness, decidedly inappropriate activity, and augmented deficiencies void of excellence.

Not any more. Let's replace the excuses. Let's replace them with better people.

People, while made of chemicals, are far more valuable than the sum of their compounded biological and chemical parts. Workers are not elements alone, so let's stop treating our employees as though their product substances and related functions were all that mattered.

Build an effective work group on more than scientific mixtures—build it on principles and values, and build your people in the process. Look to the art world for examples. Indeed, both art and science have definitive frameworks, but one acknowledges and encourages creative innovation while the other seeks to stifle or at the very least control it. There is no room for flexibility when combining certain chemicals. The same elements, united in the same quantity, will always produce the same effect. Not so with human interaction and with art.

To foster growth and creativity in a work environment, unite people normally not deemed productive, and watch them break that mold. Give them the right value and decision frameworks upon which they can agree, and they can become positively dynamic to the extreme (in the best sense of the word) if they want to. Bottom line: their "wanting to" is the key. Present them with stronger reasons to desire camaraderie than inappropriate validation for when they think they can't stand each other, and a new and more workable solution just may be the result.

When two or more diverse folks are equally committed to common values and solutions, the blending of their gifts and persons produce stronger alliances and better results. This consideration is all about decisions and desires, the reasons behind the decisions. Better blending requires a superior blender. The leader's job is to design and implement environments of mixing, where good decisions based on commitment to agreed values permeate all. Here, creativity enhances what otherwise discontented and disgruntled people would likely crush.

This isn't a book about science…it's a book about selection of atmospheres, attitudes, and actions that contribute to providing best environments where all participants can grow, contribute and prosper. How the selection takes place determines whether the result is industrial strength solution provision or dissolution and disconnect.

In the chemistry of the post-modern office, solutions—the mixing of people, personalities, work styles, relationships, mannerisms, practices of communication, ages, cultures, perspectives, motives, methods of task accomplishment, timing, tempers, experience, education, world-view, values, perceptions, problem-solving outlooks, attitudes, aptitudes and actions—all get plunged into a beaker together. Sometimes these combinations work of their own accord, but most of the time the combinations require a lot of work to create an atmosphere where participants can contribute out of strength of agreement.

Instability vs. Steady Ability—it need not be a struggle in deciding and providing which of these two shall govern, even though it often is. Unstable atmospheres can become environments of ordered motion when a tempering agent is blended in with the whole, some activator that calms the inevitability of explosion and encourages more tranquil and positive-focus interaction. The leader's job is to discover this agent, infuse it in a way that others see as desirable, and accomplish the process with as much clarity and as little confusion as possible, within a framework that stimulates agreement and implementation. The desire is to calm a stormy sea, not make more waves, to attract the fish and not scare them away.

The process is difficult, but probable. In fact, if done correctly, it will produce superb results. Groups of people that may not meld together on the surface can become great mixers if given right motives, methods, and motivation to merge well.

Office Chemistry 101A is a quick course in defining and using some of the tools and techniques to combine quality elements for good results if used properly. Yes, certain conditions have to be present to assure the best success options; these are the necessary prerequisites for achieving the goal of creating productive environments. The solutions to problems become possible when the "solutions"—the mixing of people who constitute a greater and more productive fusion—work together to create environments in which the whole group participates freely.

What is the agent that brings diverse groups together to accomplish great things, often in spite of negative circumstances? It is nothing more than *desire*.

Stir the Pot

Obligatory requirements, interwoven deadlines, audits, taxes, imposed old and new regulations, heightened customer expectations—all these are matters of profound influence on business, and produce expected circumstances with which organizations deal daily. The faster that communication methodologies force businesses to deliver or react to customer or regulatory demands, the more intense is the responsibility to make sure that the dedication to rapid response doesn't replace the sincerity of heart and the true initiative born not merely of obligation, but imbued as a part of service opportunity.

Business may move at formerly unimaginable speeds of connectivity, but people still move at the pace of the heart, and it shall forever be so. Leaders and great teams know this and employ methods that serve their staff, which serve the customer and fulfill requirements of business out of strength of desire, as opposed to conveyance of production alone.

How? Leaders stir the pot. Leaders know that circumstances like those above are going to be integral parts of regular regimen, so leaders who want to prove that character and decisions count use the evident to gain the paramount. Leaders encourage stirring the pot, the mixing of regular work requirements into broader life engagements—including matching the problems with opportunities for growth, and challenges and confrontations with possibilities for positive changes in the daily work experience.

Leaders want to see how people they lead deal with the obligatory. Life at work never is going to be smooth, because it can't be. The reality is that stresses, changes, pushes and shoves enter, usually uninvited, all the time, and incessantly grind the workplace and its participants. Leaders know this, and use common occurrences to advantage, to see character revealed and developed in the people who, if their desires are strong enough, create solutions that countermand and exceed the requirements of the circumstance. It isn't that leaders foster problems to gain solutions—far from it. Leaders know that problems come, that it's just a matter of time, and it may be today when the problems come to fruition in your department. So, since the chances are 100% that just around the next corner will be the first onslaught of the week (and it's only Monday at 6:45 a.m.), the leader forewarns, forearms, and works forward with the group to anticipate, prepare, engage, and if possible proactively solve a problem before it even occurs.

Telling people what's coming is the first job of the leader. Allowing them to create actions to counteract negatives is where the pot is stirred. People who want to grow know, because their leader has shown them, that it is their responsibility to actively participate in building solutions born of a mind-set of a "we can solve this" attitude. Desire is produced from chosen attitudes of confidence in facing what is sure to come. Desire is the stabilizing agent that causes people who may on the surface not be expected to work well together, to meld, and through their intentional mixing create workable solutions to what otherwise would be insoluble situations, at least at first.

The pot is stirred with needful information. Indeed, accurate and timely dissemination of facts serves as a collection of implements that are used to mix the ingredients, and these stir sticks can take many forms. The leader's job is to:

• *Teach.* Instruction that is received alters perspective—it has to. It may confirm already held beliefs, or open doors to new ones. Regardless, when a leader teaches that teacher-leader stirs the pot, new ideas are introduced, traditional concepts challenged, knowledge bases widened. As the stirring occurs, those anchored well will remain with their weight on solid ground; those who float will likely be skimmed off of the surface. These may not be discarded, but placed into another solution where they can be tried again. If a leader skims and still sees value in the residue, one of the strongest contributions that leader can make is to offer a second chance to those who would like to withstand and grow; if correction and re-placement is received, there is hope.

- *Warn.* Clear and expected danger might only be revealed from the leader's perspective. If the leader says nothing, disaster could strike, and swiftly. Warnings don't automatically cause groups to change their behavior; they present facts and data that if taken seriously could cause behaviors to change because the people want to change in light of what they have learned. Desire as the agent is seen in the active role of bringing people together to face challenges directly and decisively.

- *Direct.* When the decision has to be made and the leader has to make it, he or she does, period. Confident decision-making directs energies and activities toward expected results that come from cooperation on a course of action known or believed to be right. Firm direction comes from solid motives and applied wisdom based on solid ideals and values. Direction helps groups see and avoid danger or points ways to avert disaster and solve issues, and is essential for survival and to stimulate growth. Direction gives group members contexts in which their solutions become reality.

- *Reinforce.* Grow confidence through encouragement. A leader who sees his or her people winning through struggle will not be aloof; that leader will align and engage with them because the leader knows his or her presence and pro-action matter greatly. Genuine offers of encouragement have to come from one who is attached, and affirmation is best received when these attachments are strong. Perhaps to those observing from the extremities this would not appear to be the kind of interaction that stirs and dishevels, but encouragement that sees the big picture offers assurance and hope through the difficulties, and fights on behalf of the one who needs help, further engaging when giving up might otherwise be considered a viable alternative. Encouragement stirs the pot because it transforms perspectives and motivates for endurance.

- *Correct.* A leader will not be content with recurring error on the parts of the leader or the team and will look for right opportunities to properly address incidents (activities, events) that indicate issues (reasons behind the occurrences) where values are being violated or function is being hindered by inappropriate behaviors, lack of needful resources, or imbalance between relationship and function. The leader is not a cop; he or she is a coach, and the coach understands the game so well, likely has played many of the roles before, that he or she is in a best position to help point out mistakes, realign activity with values and goals, and help the team participant move to greater levels of accomplishment as errors are owned, forgiveness demonstrated, and renewed motivation results.

• *Reaffirm.* Restate and uphold the motive. Whether in an environment of hope or despair, success or failure, regularly restating the reason for which a group is involved in any worthwhile project pushes people who really want its fulfillment, to work all the more to get it. Those who laugh or loiter may soon be seen as shallow and superficial when the motive's reiteration calls others who are dedicated to access and employ reserves they didn't know they had, and engage in actions they didn't realize they could perform.

• *Congratulate.* Recognize and affirm the wins. Why should affirmation stir the pot? It does because it indicates whether the leader's praise is an anomaly or part of the anatomy of the health of the organization, and it shows if the recipient is humble enough to receive honest and heart-felt congratulations. It is more blessed to give than to receive, and when done with integrity, both are pretty hard to accomplish without undue pride—hence the struggle. The pot is stirred when the affirmation is genuinely expressed from the heart, with the sole intent to build up authentically, and the receiver accepts the praise with humility. Character is challenged to accepting gracefully, and with gratitude. Those who won't connect with themselves and others in this endeavor are hiding, and stirring this pot reveals them and causes them to consider needful change, and hopefully stimulates their desires to do so.

Light the Flame

Heat is the energy produced by randomly moving particles. Heat is also an energized atmosphere that is created when people are moved, either in an ordered fashion or within disorderly motion, because their circumstances change, or designs fostered upon them necessitate change. Whether people will or war against change, they are positioned or repositioned to accomplish new and improved results that remaining static simply cannot produce.

Leaders accept heat and, at times, generate it. In fact, although they may not desire it if it comes as an unwelcome guest, they encourage endurance when it does come because the rising temperatures tell the true stories of character and quests to remain strong, regardless. Problems solved in high intensity moments become success markers that prepare winners to win again, fully prepared for when the next contest comes, and the heat is on once more.

It is amazing to see what remains when voracious fires engulf and destroy homes. In these very sad events the most enduring items are the ones that withstand and outlast the intensity of the highest temperatures the onslaughts produce. Fireplaces and chimneys rising as lone sentinels after a firestorm has swept through remind observers that they were once conductors utilized to control the very force that consumed what formerly existed around them.

In a work environment when pressures intensify and the heat is turned up, a leader looks for those stronger characters that will withstand, and remain standing, who endure because they continue to be conductors of force under proper control, proven through crises. Controlled heat is a blessing on a cold night. Leaders welcome heat when it promises comfort, and accept it when it portends challenge, teaching others how to control it, so it doesn't control them.

Expect to See Differences: Nothing Will Be the Same

If you are the leader and you stir the pot, or are present on a team when the circumstances provide heated impetus for a stirring to occur, you will allow, if not promote, this activity within the group for purposed and right reasons: to produce character and endurance and prepare for greater challenges. Wins come against odds, not when the opposition doesn't show. It is upon a win over obstacles that you can expect results that will permanently alter a work environment and deeply impact your leadership substance and style as well as your team's opportunities for expanded output. This is the beginning of industrial strength solutions.

If you are the leader, or a follower who is or wants to be fully engaged, then you will see varied evidences of effective mixing when the pot is stirred, regardless of who holds the stirrer. Some of the more negative indicators may include:

1. Some will question why a leader "allowed" an event or series of them to occur, questioning motive and method.
2. Others will cower and simply ditch efforts to become occupied in solution provision, whining as they run.
3. Others will hide, fearing recrimination, demotion or demolition of their careers, status, or positions.
4. Others will cite enhanced risk that is perceived to be greater than reward and will shrink from adversity.
5. Others will blame anyone close by in efforts to diffuse their own culpability or laziness.
6. Others will try to create alignments of "people who feel the same way" and will dissolve before your eyes when you ask them to name "those people."
7. Others will write anonymous notes because they don't have the courage to sign their own names.
8. Others will play the victim because it is in that state where they believe they are noticed more readily, and this act becomes their sole route to designing a form of

"recognition" that does not prove to be even close to credible.

9.   Others will commit to their courses with lukewarm energy because they connive to steal time and other people's energy to serve their own purposes, and then justify these actions.
10.   Others will lie, steal, cover up, and then seek cover.
11.   Others will delegate responsibility to subordinates they know will have little chance of success, and so excuse their failures with the delegating-authority disclaimer: "I told you so."
12.   Others will seek to live in fault finding, whining, and whimpering.
13.   Others simply will abandon the leader and the cause for which the leader and the leader's organization stand. Maybe they should.

Stirring the pot will demonstrate these attributes of unhealthy character in those who do not have the desire for growth, or wish to undermine someone else's maturity or advancement. It forces the worst elements to the surface. Call them what they are: inhibitors, brake pedals, and roadblock builders. They will be not unlike a race horse that never gets out of the gate when the starting gun sounds, or lags behind all the others and becomes the loser, yes, but potentially a noteworthy loser to boot—probably getting way too much attention because the loss is great and the neighing abusively loud.

Team members who skim the surface will be skimmed from the surface in time, largely because they choose this reaction by their own actions. A leader must remove or replace those who destruct because they refuse to construct. Too much is at stake to not take corrective and decisive measures. This is often easier said than done, and if it is done, a competent leader will perform the difficult duties with respect, dignity, truthfulness and integrity. Where there is an opportunity for redemption, the leader will create places for re-institution, or a re-initiation of beginning successes, and encourage development within a continuum of constant evaluation. But it takes a penitent and willing person to own errors in this engagement, cease being his or her own victim, learn from the experience, and grow.

A leader wants success for the ones that are led and will see that, when the pot is stirred and changes are coming, the stirring helps develop potential. Leaders do not avoid tumult regardless of its source—generally it can't be avoided anyway—it has to be faced. Stirring reveals those who want to win, or who want to know how to participate in activities that have best opportunities for success. Adversity points up quality strengths and quantified commitments of those who believe in the value of dedicated effort and practice it regardless of discomfort, hard work, sweat, or loss.

Among these winning people are those who, although they may not see the whole picture, try to make their parts better through their contributions in fulfilling their tasks, whether noticed or not. They are faithful to accomplish their pieces, and in doing so create resiliency and encouragement for others to accomplish their responsibilities. These are the courageous ones who look for durable solutions because they care enough to submit their perceived comfort to a greater cause of credibility. These people evaluate risks, and act on higher motives even if the costs are monumental.

These people don't dwell in blame or finding fault; they forgive and move on and usually up. They refuse associations with discouragers and malcontents—and they certainly won't try to change them. Their energies are reserved for supporting those who, with diligence, survive, strive and thrive.

These are people of integrity who possess ownership, theirs most of all. Not content to mask their errors, they admit to them and refuse to wallow in a quagmire of quintessential guilt. They clarify issues, accept forgiveness and if it is not offered, forgive their own selves. They are finished with disasters in an unfortunate past, and although having learned from them, refuse to live in their negative remembrances and draining effects. They own their duties with full disclosure and declare their intentions openly. Then they follow through and complete their jobs.

The CTRG Boxes

Richard Willis is a friend and a client of Creative Team Resources Group, Inc. (www.ctrg.com). Richard has created what he calls, "CTRG Boxes." As a result of a stirring of the pot, he literally makes lists of the actions he needs to take to become a more productive contributor, puts a box to the left of each item, and does not consider closure of action to have occurred until each CTRG box is checked. That is follow-through that works, and is the mark of growing individuals who decide to benefit from organizational change.

Stirring the pot reveals true characters and their characteristics and more. The leader's job is to observe, remember, report, and act, knowing that when any trouble comes, the results will be known and nothing will be the same. Change will be inevitable. Further, the leader and the team agree that they will be prepared for all that is coming in a future quest for assured victory.

The Encounter

Leadership of a team that longs for workable solutions, a mix of talents, gifts, strong relationships, capabilities and abilities, seeks to discover and draw out the best in those who follow. Whenever and wherever a need for help is noticed the leader who wants the team to work well will extend his or her assistance, and while not owning the success of the followers, certainly contributes to their successes by supplying helps that only a leader may be able to give.

Such was the case on February 27, 2005, for my wife, our son and me. We were visiting Washington, D.C. with dear friends, and were privileged to attend church services at St. John's Church, across the street from Lafayette Park. The service was to begin at 8:00 a.m., and we were told that President and Mrs. Bush might be in attendance that day. We were, of course, excited at this prospect, and arrived at the church a little before 7:00 a.m. It was unbelievably cold and I surmised that the Secret Service had compassion on us, allowing us to pass through security and get into the warm building perhaps sooner than anyone anticipated.

There were six in our party and we were seated one row in back of another, three-and-three, about 10 rows from the front on an aisle. We realized that we were the only ones presently in the church, except for one Secret Service agent who sat two rows in back of us, and an occasional parade of other agents, White House staff, and a couple of ushers who moved through, up and down the aisles. As the clock neared 7:30 a.m. the church began to fill, and at about 7:50 a.m. the lone agent left his seat and knelt in the aisle by my side, greeted me warmly, and asked if my wife would kindly move her coat to the other side of our son, which I communicated to her, and she did. He thanked me, and left. Odd, I thought, but we were not ones to question at that point.

Several minutes later, just before 8:00 a.m., Mrs. Bush, followed by President Bush, entered from stage left (audience right) at the front of the church and greeted the clergy. My first thought was, "They look just like they do on TV." Duh. Only one other time had I had the opportunity to be in the same room with a president, actually George W. Bush's father, when he had come to San Diego to speak to our downtown Rotary club, and I only saw him from a distance away.

Our assumption was that President and Mrs. Bush would sit toward the front of the church, so when they walked across the front, turned left and proceeded down the aisle toward us, we were startled, if not taken aback. But we were completely amazed when Mrs. Bush sat directly behind my wife, Cindy, and the President sat directly in back of me. I suddenly became acutely aware of the back of my head, and hoped my haircut and coat collar were okay! Understand that St. John's church was constructed in 1820, and that people may have been a little shorter back then, and that these pews had been placed very close together. To be that near a president dwarfed any other experience with notable folks I had ever met, let me tell you. In fact, in my talks since this event occurred, I am fond of saying that if you have ever had a leader breathe down your neck, I can top that!

The service proceeded, and President and Mrs. Bush were fully engaged in the liturgy. From the Book of Common Prayer we were led, responded, quoted Scripture and prayed. As part of this outline we were presented with the opportunity to "stand and greet one another" and all in our party gulped, then smiled. We rose and noticed that the first people the President and Mrs. Bush greeted warmly and with great enthusiasm were a group of teenagers sitting to our right, expressing engaged interest in them as would, well, people who were truly interested. Then we met the First Couple. Warm and gracious, they put us at ease as I introduced my family to them, and I noticed particularly how intentional President Bush was in his gaze, and firm in his handshake.

The service progressed and the homily concluded, at which time the President addressed Laura and said, "That was good," (and it was). The congregation was given the option at this time of participating in a segment of the service called Communion. At this service the communion elements are served at an altar at the front of the church, and those who wish to partake file up to take their kneeling places there, to be served by two of the clergy, one with the wafer representing the body of Christ, and one with the wine, representing His blood shed for redemption of sin, the wine served from a common chalice.

It came time for our row to proceed and we stood, as did the President and Mrs. Bush who were in back of us. Turning to him,

I thought it only proper that I offer that he and Mrs. Bush proceed first, seeing that he is the most powerful man in the world, and his response was, "No, no, you and your friends go first," which we did. I mean, you don't really want to argue with a president, right? So I let my wife go first, followed by my son, and as I was about to proceed up the aisle as well, I felt a deliberate tugging at my right coat pocket, a pulling on the fabric that was clearly intentional. I looked quickly back and surmised immediately that it could be none other than George W. Bush—no one else was near. Indeed, it was he. My coat pocket flap had become tucked into the pocket, askew to the world, and he simply reached out— and fixed my coat. It was a moment. While knowing exactly what had happened I wasn't sure exactly why, but in looking into his face, was greeted by shining eyes and a huge grin. He said, verbatim, "I just want you to look sharp going up there." All I could do was smile and say, "Why, thank you, Mr. President." What would you say? Stunned as I was, and as I think about it still, I recall feelings now of a combination of gratitude, amazement, and light-hearted friendly encounter, all enveloped into one moment in time.

We proceeded up to the front altar, and the President and I knelt side by side for communion. I was served first, and then we both bowed in silent prayer after taking the elements. One of the pictures that my wife carries in her mind and describes so well is that as she was finished praying she looked up, and will always remember seeing Glen Aubrey and the President of the United States kneeling together in prayer at an altar of communion.

Clearly this is a great memory for us, and because there were no cameras, media, or other devices to record such a moment, the event lives and is cherished in our minds, and will for as long as our recollections last. What a privilege!

But there are lessons here, important leadership and team-building lessons. From that encounter forward I have reflected on them substantially and will highlight them here. See if they ring true in light of what you have just read:

1. Leadership that commands respect is fully engaged in and with the people who follow, regardless of station or status.
2. Leadership whole-heartedly participates through a team's function where strong relational values permeate understanding, and cooperation on behalf of a cause perpetuates right action.
3. Leadership is intentional and not distracted by non-essentials.
4. Leadership is complimentary.
5. Leadership is firm in its commitment toward a higher and worthwhile purpose.
6. Leadership looks for ways to make followers successful, even if it means invading. In the story above, simply making my coat look appropriate was a service rendered by the President that he did not have to do! He did it, though, for the reasons he stated, and I was the beneficiary.
7. Leadership is humble and submissive to a Creator and a Cause greater than self. Kneeling in prayer at an altar before God in obedience to His authority says much about the man and his wife, politics notwithstanding. Humble leaders serve to the best of their God-given abilities when they recognize the Source from which their strength comes.

If you are the leader or a follower on a working team who is fortunate enough to be engaged in activities with a leader of this kind, accent these positive attributes from a heart of gratitude and grow with that leader who is one you emulate and respect. Every team member may not agree with every facet of functionality in which the team engages, but great teams who strive to be part of and create solutions that work, possess strong and maturing relationships, and these are their prime encouragements and motivations for success. Cooperation on a team, where leader and followers labor together from shared perspectives toward common goals with servant-hearted attitudes and actions, produces superior results and likely changed lives for the better. Ours were.

Character is not chemically controlled; it is chosen even in the surprising, pot-stirring or heat-enhancing times. Chance adversity, or the intentional stirring of the pot, or a heating of the elements, will never allow the people mixture to revert to its original state. In human behavior and endeavor too much will have been seen, too much action devolved, too many character choices known; participants who desire best results will never be content to go back, or remain the same when change and challenge force realignment of thoughts and actions.

Improvement is the result of stirring information that alters the handling of circumstances, revealing new opportunities for people to become better should they so choose. To create industrial strength solutions, the leader and the team look to create and wholeheartedly participate in deliberate and solution-oriented processes especially for the benefit of the group, knowing that the greater good will be served if the goals are achieved.

One of the first processes to consider is turning whining into winning. Not an easy assignment, but one upon which we will focus next.

Chapter 2:
Winning vs. Whining

The Teacher

Jack was a friend, a gentleman much older than I. He was a WWII Veteran, having fought in battles I had only read about. I am a baby-boomer, so WWII and the events surrounding it would always be a study for me and not a lived experience. Yet, somehow, as on occasion I had opportunity to view Jack, watch him work, and hear his philosophical pronouncements, I was given opportunity to "live" in his experiences as I sought to learn from the life lessons he taught, and there were many.

He was a tradesman. After the War's conclusion he decided to settle, start a family, and chose what was to become my neck of the woods as his domicile. I first met him in a non-profit charitable organization where he won me over with his smile and accent—decidedly southern, and genuine. His interest in me, I have concluded since, did not originate in shared abilities—we were very different from one another. Rather, it originated in our mutual understanding of service with quality behind the scenes—we mutually tried to contribute with excellence whether anyone noticed or not. Our hidden-from-the-applause efforts were those we didn't speak about; somehow talking about or dwelling too much on what we had done could, or would, sacrifice the purity of any good or best motive in the earnest methods of an endeavor, if not the endeavor itself. Accenting humility would somehow cause that humility to lose its full impact and become not so humble any more. So, we both just "knew." Jack helped me, and I helped him to the extent that I could, and I always admired his diligence and desire to serve.

His trade was that of electrician. I was one of those who knew enough about electricity to leave it alone, and by the time I met Jack I had already fried at least one screwdriver. Clearly this was a field in which I should walk as an observer and only at a distance. During this time we developed several electrical installation needs at our home, so I asked Jack if he would come and do the work, fully intending to pay him what I would have paid any other electrician.

Jack was always on time. I struggled in this area. He showed me the value of commitment through his example, and I learned and tried to put his model into practice. I watched him work. I saw him struggle. I saw him get hurt while climbing over beams to run wire. Remember, he was a WWII Veteran, and this was the 1980's. He was "old" by my age standards, and I wanted to make sure he didn't slip or fall. However, watching him and hearing him, I realized I was the one who would slip and fall before he ever would...in principles, character, right standing, and commitments. So we both hung on.

One particular day in what was turning out to be a "larger than expected" wiring job for which I was "hiring" him (he refused payment at the end) he was embattled mightily with a wire run that would have challenged anyone regardless of age or ability. It was a hot day, oppressively so, and Jack was sweating like a shower. I wanted to help, and while telling him of my intentions, and trying to lend a hand there was no way I could really be of any significant assistance—there was room for only one where he was sandwiched—so I mainly tried to keep out of the way, steady the ladder, and offer him cold drinks when he would come down and shake off the dust. At one point in his efforts while aloft in the crawl space, and probably not aware I could hear him, he made a comment I will forever remember. It was this, addressed with intent and firm commitment to the wire with which he was having so much trouble, inconvenience and discomfiture: "I'm gonna win—I'm gonna win." And in due time, he did, yes, did he ever. That installation, his installation, remains well into the 2000's and needs no improvement.

Years passed. Jack and his family moved to the Deep South. He had retired and wanted to go to the place of his roots. One of the peculiar incidents of life then occurred, a juxtaposition of people, places and times that upon review and contemplation contribute to cherished memories. I was invited to be the speaker at a series of training sessions for his son-in-law, one of my dearest friends. Upon accepting the invitation I asked if Jack might attend any of the sessions—it would be good to see him. You see, in the intervening years he had contracted cancer, and while never forfeiting his optimism, he was suffering and all knew that the battle would draw to a close in time.

It was a special and tender moment when, after one seminar, Jack came up to speak to me. I had seen him in the audience, and my countenance must have alluded to the fact that I was glad he was there, because I was, sincerely. When we met in person down front we greeted each other warmly. The same deep respect I had felt so many years before seemed even more a gift I desired to give back. This was a great man who at this time was physically struggling, and bearing his condition well. We spoke of his disease and I asked him how he was doing. Without reservation he described the pain, but through his confident comments he made it clear that he had decided his discomfort was not going to be his focus…unbelievably, his focus was centered on me. Out of high regard I ventured only as far as I thought appropriate in discussing his health and prognosis. At one point, he seemed to let down a bit…and ventured comments, describing that the cancer was getting him, and he knew it.

It was a poignant moment. I said, "Jack…let me remind you of something that may encourage you." I reminded him about the wiring job, the difficulty, the stress of the installation, the commitment he showed and his outstanding positive attitude. He remembered. Then I said, "Jack, when the job was so tough that most men would have cursed it and the guy who hired them, you addressed the wire." He looked puzzled. "You spoke to the wire," I stated it differently, and some of the confusion in his face dissolved. "Jack," I said, "Remember what you said? You said: 'I'm gonna win, I'm gonna win.' And you did!" His understanding was greater than mine. I sought conclusion but his was already enveloping my next comment: "In this current challenge, my friend, remember what you said. You will win…you will win." Eyes glistened, tears followed, we gave each other a hug, and we parted.

It was several months later when Jack died. But clearly, he had won. He had shown a younger friend who needed the lesson and the encouragement how to win in difficult times and uncomfortable circumstances, and had taken it upon himself to win again, no matter the odds. His win is seen in the strong legacy he left—in his family, his extended family, and one friend who is older now, who watched him work on a hot day with a challenging electrical installation where character and fortitude were evidenced in strong measure, and resiliency of character won the day. Jack, you were then, and are now, a true inspiration. You, sir, are a winner.

What makes a winner? Further, what is the difference between winning and whining? Well, as you can assuredly imagine it is much more than the choice and rearrangement of the letters of the alphabet that form the words. However, were the differences reduced to only that, just take out an "h" and throw in another "n" and you've got it. Playing with the letters and the words they could represent, just remove your despairing and droning Hum of "Woe is me" and throw in a confident "'No way I'm gonna be beat"...and you have obliterated the possibility or propensity of whining, at least in the spelling. But replacing whining with winning in real life application involves much more than words alone.

Whining was so far removed from Jack's character that I would imagine no one, or at most very few, heard a "woe is me" peep uttered from his lips, ever. Maybe the whining, if there ever was any, was masked by his dedication to showcase a high degree of courtesy and character, and present a different and stronger ethic of endurance and energy. These characteristics may have come from, and been strengthened by the events of a not-so-removed and yet somewhat distant time of intense international struggle in which he played and contributed his part with determination and skill. Those who fought in WWII were indeed the Great Generation and I for one am exceedingly grateful for their contributions on many levels. What fortitude and faithfulness they modeled, demonstrating traits that so many of the United States military have emulated in multiple, severe and trying conflicts since! Thanks to all of them for their service and sacrifice!

There are those today who face strong adversaries and adversity, who bear their trials well, conquer fully, or are consumed trying. Therefore, we must conclude that winning is a choice as must be whining also. Whining or winning: simply, it's a choice based on desire for the design of the outcome. The choice to whine originates in atmospheres where blame and lack of ownership of responsibility are tolerated or encouraged. The decision to win originates from a character that is born and bred to endure through trial. It is raised and brought up, dedicated and therefore destined not to be subjugated to changing circumstances, but to face them, move through them, learn from them, and grow beyond them, leaning forward to next levels of maturity and development.

Losers whine, and wallow in sorrow. Winners work— toward a better tomorrow. Whiners love to drag complainers with them into the quagmire of their superficial undertakings. Winners lead, and others who want to win follow enthusiastically and wholeheartedly. They see the results of great choices to rise above inconvenience and mature through adversity. It's a stark comparison: winning through focused endeavor, pro-active engagement, and accompanying victory, versus a whiner's shallow and slothful abandonment seen in sheer recalcitrance or a plaintive showcase of ineptitude or negative attitude when they continue to, well, just whine.

The term "whining" begs for its particular definition. Try this one: whining is a state of desperation where dwelling in defeat and declaring it, is its own reward. Whiners repine so others know the whiner is dwelling in the clutches of misery. Whiners permeate their surroundings, sometimes employing elongated tones of desolation, despondency, despair, and disconnect, and then wonder why few remain near when their moaning lingers and their volume increases. "NO WHINING!" proclaimed the sign on the door of a CEO's office, facing those who were exiting. I asked him, "Does it work?" His answer: "No, it really doesn't." Too bad—maybe it was his leadership.

Telling others not to whine without offering them an alternative is like telling a starving man that you hope he gets something to eat, that he really should eat, that eating would be good for him, that he would feel better if he did eat something, that he would become more productive with the energy the food would provide, but offering him no food or no way to get it!

Whining has to be replaced with a better alternative, or it will re-fill its own void and never leave at all. Winning, and the attitudes, desires and decisions that accompany the choice to partake in its aptitude, will replace and overfill the void of whining every time. Winning is a better position because the human make-up is filled, and sustains even greater capacity, when winning replaces whining. Whining is a cheapened and demeaning experience for its owner, and begs to be gotten rid of.

Winning is a rewarding and effectual method of fully living, and it yearns for others to duplicate it and relish its victory.

Who would you rather have on your team, a group of winners or whiners? More to the point, would you rather be a winner or whiner, and with whom would you prefer to serve if you are the follower?

Let's be candid: the act of replacing attitudes of whining with declared perspectives of winning can be tough—in fact, the leader can't do it for anyone else but the leader, and the follower only for the follower. To each are his or her personal choices and actions to change negative perspectives into positive ones. In short, the whiners have to do it for themselves! That being said how is it then even possible that a whiner would have motivation enough to start to think and act like a winner?

Try this thought, and see if it sticks: the way a whiner can convince him or her self to win is to willfully change his or her perspective because the desire is cultivated to do so. Or, stated alternatively, the desire for better is larger than the desire for bitter. The way a perspective can change is if he or she has been shown something more preferable than current misery and, because of the goal, wants to move to something beyond indolence and complacency. Alterations in perspectives are possible through receptivity of new information, if the receiver is open. If a receptor is closed, then a person is blind to possibility, and remains fomenting a current condition of unhappiness and ineptitude.

If a current condition is one of struggle, victimization, or "feeling sorry for myself" then whining is most likely what is heard from its occupant. The dweller in the cellar who hates where he or she is but is unwilling to cease whining long enough to consider climbing the stairs to reach the light of day is not a person upon whom a leader can build industrial strength solutions, nor is that person one upon whom team members can count for positive change. Leaders and team members who win look for winners—others who want to grow from and through circumstances. If you are a team participant who engages in whining, become a winner and build for something better, and live and contribute in strength.

Where to begin? There are four solid decisions a whiner can make based on a new perspective if the whiner wants to become a winner. The individual, regardless of station or title, who wants to win and to continue his or her upward momentum, can and will repeatedly make these decisions and enjoy the results.

The Four Decisions

1. *Turn habits of complaining into habitats of construction.*

This is more than wishful thinking—this is hard decision-making. A habit is a behavioral pattern that is well entrenched and may have taken years to build, so it will not be undone without dedicated efforts and just plain hard work.

A decision to live differently is only verified when action follows that says the decision to construct a new habitat was intentional; behaviors change, and atmospheres follow suit. Results are seen as decisions become evidenced in real life application, so until a behavior changes, decisions are words only.

The process of making a decision to change a habit weighs choices and their consequences. Consideration "A" may show the decision maker that upon making better choices, to win and not to whine, certain positive results can be expected over time, and are worth the risk of change. Consideration "B" will show the decision maker that if he or she continues down the current path of complaint and self-doubt, the same results within a current habitat will simply be repeated. Consequences tell the truth of the results of a decision—the path-chooser makes the decisions on the basis of what he or she wants. Again, it all boils down to desire. "What do you want?" is the question that frames the difference between being content in losing or insatiable in the desire for winning.

Whining will be replaced with winning only if and when the focus based on desire changes, if the desire for constructing a more positive habitat is stronger than the complacency of the current existence. Often keeping this focus in front of the mind, just remembering the decision, is tough. Tools may be needed to assist. And there is nothing wrong with using tools! Ones that are designed by you or ones designed by others—if they work and are right, use them. This book could be a tool, refrigerator reminders, photos, images, songs, rituals, group encouragements, meetings with friends for strengthening commitments and owning accountability—the list is long. Whatever tool you may need to become committed to replacing whining with winning, as long as it works and doesn't violate principle or other people, go for it.

Whining creeps up and exercises insidious influence. It moves stealthily upon an unsuspecting victim and, before you know it, consumes. This happens because there is a tendency within the human psyche to blame someone or something else before owning responsibility of one's actions. Regardless of the source of that leaning, the fact is that it is there. So if one wants to replace whining with winning, one will own responsibility, and remember to do so, regardless. Hence the need for tools, "remembering devices" that refresh the memory of the reasons and benefits for an attitude to be developed that is centered on a win and not a waste.

Construction will replace complaining because it says "N.O." to Needless Obstacles. Complaining at its core searches for a scapegoat, whereas construction at its core means acquiring the hammer and using it to build a structure you want, no matter the difficulty. It's the difference between hesitation and activation. The cause is desire; the result is action.

Hesitate in the action of breaking a habit, and the habit will continue to control and possibly break you. You will be in charge when you decide that the consequences of breaking the whining habit and replacing it with the desire to construct a new habitat on the winning side are worth your diligent effort, time and costs.

2. *Replace negative attitudes with positive solution-focused outlooks.*
   There are a lot of reasons to choose optimism over pessimism. One is that optimism simply feels better. Another even more important reason is that optimism provides a framework of action that sets in motion the movements designed to produce their desired good results. Optimists look to the future with hope, and hope and whining cannot co-exist.

   The negative folks among us try to convince others that dire straights are imminent, catastrophe is about to befall, the challenges are too hard, the roads too long. Simply remove yourself from their presence.

   Observe a mountain. One party sees it as an obstacle exceedingly hard to conquer; the other sees it as a platform for a vista that apart from scaling it would never even be known to exist. It's the same mountain but totally different perspectives, the same climb, but different goals. The activity of climbing this mountain will be fueled by the kinds and scopes of desires that are so strong that they see that benefits truly outweigh costs; or, out of an unwilling obligation to try to move an obstruction, resistance concludes that life is hard and it may not be worth the effort anyway, so why bother?

   A perspective drives those who gaze at opportunity, those who see viable options. That perspective views life as an adventure and living it to its fullest a fulfillment. Your attitude choices are superimposed on the processes in which you are engaged and deeply affect the quality of the life you live; infuse those processes with a positive point of view, and watch the processes themselves and the people within them, including you, benefit unequivocally from the enthusiasm that results and the energy your optimism provides.

3. *Redirect an ego-centered focus to concentrating on benefiting others.*
     There is a place for ego, and in its proper place the ego is essential to health. When how you feel about yourself is a part of your worth and dignity this realization is motivational to preservation and propagation. A misplacement of ego, however, where self-aggrandizement is the focus to the detriment of others and causes loss of well-being, is an absence of self-control and a general contributor to living in a misguided value system.
     A life's value system that appreciates little else than self-preservation, eventually will self-destruct. It is built on a faulty premise. Humans are not made to hoard and experience happiness at the same time. Humans who live in community realize that sharing is critical. The values of trust, assurance, hope, confidence, love, reliability, personal responsibility—these and others like them that are right and true are dedicated to the welfare of another and the community of all because they desire to help and not hinder. These values add worth to the one who possesses and acts upon them. These values win in large measure because they cause society to win, too.
     Non-viable traits of negative character such as the self-serving sentiments of distrust, slothfulness, unfaithfulness, jealousy, hatred—these are shared only from an ego out of bounds with a need for excessive control that manipulates and connives for its own utilitarian purposes to the detriment of others. These styles of living ultimately lose because when compared to true values they clearly are erroneous and without foundation. People with these

negative attributes most often crave avoidance of responsibility, and whining is one of the first tools they choose to make their positions known.

Misery and manipulation, when conjoined, look to find matching partners, either through propagating or alignment. They are earnest in their efforts to acquire others who will join in their loathsome camaraderie. Their intrigue and intent is to encourage multiplication of doom and gloom. A whiner instantly can be transported from feeling like a victim to causing victimization in others if allowed to.

Obviously the one who would win will call out and label an out-of-control ego for what it is, reject it, and re-direct the energy consumed in self-promotion into a contribution-focused engagement that benefits another. That re-direct becomes the pathway to winning on purpose. It brings others along with it, which is its nature, and the nature of the values that nurture its life. It regenerates itself in the community it touches. See clearly that winning and whining are both contagious, but winning lives longer and reproduces results that are desired far more than the residue left by defeat and degradation.

4. *Confront problems with positive planning and action steps.*

If you are a winning leader, be prepared. Become ready for resistance and "off the wall" comments or deeds from negative people that could incite and entice a winner on your team to start considering whining when times get tough. Exercise diligence in your efforts to point out the better choices.

Fruits of victory endure when they are passed to another generation in the form of values that live consistently and continuously in real life. New contestants in fresh challenges will still need to run their own courses, but models that have gone before can show best ways, the most conducive paths, what to avoid, and what to embrace along the journey. People who are prepared with information are better able to spot trouble before it comes upon them and then proactively participate in resolution and defuse a negative before it even has time to materialize.

If you've been accustomed to whining, and want to win, start to think like a winner. Thinking like the person you want to become sets the stage for the new and progressive roles you are to play. So plan the roles. Realize that tough and rough stuff will be portions of your transition from whiner to winner: it's a guarantee, just like the sun coming up tomorrow, it will happen. Since that is true, know, and engage.

Negative circumstances or the people connected to them can come across as unusual, perhaps bizarre, totally unbelievable, and at times surprising to the person who is dedicated in desire and design to winning. When the winner understands that a part of the metamorphosis from whining includes development of clear objectives and broadened views as to the causes of stress, that new winner is more prepared to recognize imminent signs of trouble and deal with them from a positive outlook position, so that before the temptations to whine materialize, the problems are confronted and solved and are on their ways toward strong resolutions.

Of course, it may not be that easy and often is very hard, but the preparation to avoid whining and replace it with winning is surprisingly possible, which may be why it is so seldom applied in advance—no one thinks about it. In the real world, nothing is taken for granted in becoming ready for life's pulls and pushes—especially when the directions to which they point are right. Vigilance is required of every winner, and is a developing trait of every person who wants to become one.

Winning concentrates on knowing its opposition so well that conquering may be repeated, regardless of circumstances. It never underestimates its adversaries, especially the unscrupulous ones like unfaithfulness, jealousy, dishonesty and hatred that when activated become destructive to the very person who employs their misguided motives.

Winning vs. Whining—this really is no contest in terms of preference for a person who wants to be part of, and contribute to, an industrial strength solution. There is, however, a conquest for and with the person over the ruling negatives, who wants to instigate this important uplifting change in lifestyle and character and replace negatives with positives.

Good change is a procedure of transformation based on information and desire for better results. It comes into being over time, when a person who becomes discontented with blaming others searches for truer fulfillment that can only come when ownership of responsibility, forward-prepared and purposeful thinking and dedication to action alter behavior. Because a former whiner wants his or her behavior to change for the better, in view of the process of winning and the rewards that are sure to follow, the new winner soon realizes that accomplishment comes to and through the person who willfully changes. That person chooses well who uses the four decisions as a guide.

The Four Decisions
Turning Whining into Winning

Turn habits of complaining into habitats of constructing.	**Replace** negative attitudes with positive solution-focused outlooks.	**Redirect** an ego-centered focus to concentrating on benefiting others.	**Confront** problems with positive planning and action steps.

Chapter 3:
Nitpicking and Petty Criticism

Crows and Red-tailed Hawks are both fairly common fowl in Southern California. From our backyard we often observe their interactive air-borne antics. For example, when crows' nests appear to be threatened by the hawks, the crows, with sudden determination, become mightily emboldened in their attempts to protect their habitat and families, diligent in their collective efforts to drive the un-welcomed intruders away. Crows will attack the hawks that threaten their living spaces by lunging and picking at them repeatedly in flight, sometimes with two or three crows engaging one hawk, until the hawk decides that easier accommodations and hunting grounds might be found elsewhere, and departs. Interestingly, the crows don't seem to really hurt the hawks, but the annoyance factor must be huge, as is the noise from both species.

In a way, related to lunging and picking, a nitpicker in a work group may begin as a discontented and distrusting individual who continually feels that his or her space and place are threatened by more powerful people—their presence, personality or drive—or by one who simply has more command, attractive appearance or appeal. This insecure soul will, in frustration and insecurity, resort to actions that are designed to tear down, drive away, force out and eliminate the unwanted person deemed as the "intruder." The difference here, of course, is that the threat is not to life and limb at the office or in the field; rather, the threat is perceived to be to position, place, authority, money, image or responsibility, and is caused usually by envy and actions born of resentment that are the true causes behind most disgruntlement.

Petty criticism is a common first-action a nitpicker employs, perhaps not always with overt intent in the beginning, but usually derived over time where eventually intent becomes content. And upon this pettiness does a nitpicker's survival depend. Negative comments may reveal undermining purposes slowly at first, testing grounds of receptivity then escalate to points where they simply cannot be ignored, as their destructive powers are unleashed. Petty criticism is meaningless and useless, but when used as a lethal weapon in an arsenal of disparagement to undercut and destroy others' characters and competencies its combined effects can be immeasurably destructive to individuals and groups if allowed to fester and reproduce. "Petty" of course means that the criticism has in its laser beam the tiniest faults of another that when spotted are magnified beyond reasonable proportion to become targets for larger missiles of gossip, lies, innuendo, maligning intentions and other divisive and destructive activities.

Leaders and group members who desire industrial strength solutions will simply not tolerate petty criticism or nitpicking. They will stop them cold. Marginal disapprovals can soon lead to petulant dispositions, and an atmosphere of productivity can be turned into discontent and disconnect if negativism is allowed to breed. Because negativity fosters its own kind, and is only fulfilled when it has permeated every corner of the workplace, its permutation must cease. A good leader and team will confront it head on and remove it.

There is no room in building industrial strength solutions to accommodate a remaining presence of disruptive attitudes of misaligned and malcontent people. When a leader and a group become attuned to recognizing initial indicators that this insidiousness is creeping in, they know they must tear it out by its roots so it will not gain the solidarity it requires to endure. Pain notwithstanding, the cure must be accomplished.

The leader and the leader's team need to be aware of distinctive characteristics of work arena dysfunctions to be able to obliterate needless argumentation, backstabbing, and futile confrontations—the nitpicking and petty criticism of the workplace. The leader is best served, as is the group he or she serves, when all the members of the work group become educated in the recognition of these negatives and the procedures to use to eliminate these disconnecting forces when they enter the environment.

Wanton Faultfinding

The first indicator of trouble is the observable presence of petulant and pervasive faultfinding. Reckless in its application, faultfinding seeks to impose unnecessary blame for mistakes with methods of morbid discovery to unearth and exaggerate nearly every problem. Devoid of drive to discover solutions, faultfinding thrives to place and spread guilt so that central focus is mainly upon culpability and failure as opposed to purposeful solution creation and implementation. Faultfinding finds a deviant pleasure in pointing its bony accusatory finger to the person or entity perceived to have made an error, spreading the word to all who would hear. Rarely does the fault sleuth delve beyond his or her hasty conclusions of liability, no matter that more thorough investigation could reveal markedly differing reality. It's far easier to name and blame than it is to uncover true sources with declared and positive intentions of moving to discover and implement solutions.

Of course, there is a place for legitimate investigation and discovery of knowledge of the sources of difficulty or error. The difference here is this: knowledge of the source born of a solution mindset seeks a remedy to empower the players to not repeat the activity that caused the problem. Faultfinding desires to dwell in the dysfunction and its results and relishes placing the guilt, because, if aggravated enough, the results could lead to re-placement or removal of the guilty person, whether or not that action is shown to be a "best" solution. Faultfinding as an accepted or tolerated operation comprises negative posturing toward dissolution. This is a place where nitpicking and petty criticisms foster what is really desired: severance or severe, if not permanent, disconnect.

Permeated faultfinding prevents restitution, in fact, abhors it. The true insidious pleasure of a faultfinder is the "I told you so" attitude heard in words and seen in actions. Achieving the credit for knowing that someone could stumble or fall, struggle or fail becomes the motive of the misaligned member who desires that another on the team go down so that the criticizer still stands, and is noticed because of this discrepancy.

This unhealthy and misplaced competition has no room in building industrial strength solutions. The leader and the group are constantly on the lookout for wanton faultfinding, and when it occurs they won't have to struggle to notice it. When evidenced, they identify it and curtail its presence before destruction results.

Wasted Energy

So much vitality is sapped from leaders when they try repeatedly to work with someone who has little or no desire to contribute, a person who instead relishes a position of conspicuousness the dearth of good choices can create around him or her. A leader who wants to see a whiner become a winner will talk about a situation like this openly and directly with the person involved, but must realize that the leader cannot make the good decisions for the one who needs to change.

Nitpickers and petty criticizers who are allowed to continue in their demonstrations of dysfunctional behaviors will end up requiring mountains of time and energy from a leader who may be unwilling to confront misdeeds in a timely fashion, or lacks the courage to tell the truth that desperately needs to be told. Ultimately the cost of living with these vitality-sappers is far greater than that needed to make the superior choices of dealing upfront with the problem. The longer the energy is wasted or not applied appropriately in dealing with the negative issues at hand and the people who are causing them, the more the sacrifice on the rest of the team becomes needless.

Wasted energy is the result of unwillingness on the part of a leader to deal with the obvious and, when allowed to fester, breeds more of what is causing the unsettledness and its corresponding lack of production. Wasted energy becomes the leader's payment to cover his or her personal lack of courage or fear of confrontation.

Compassion for an erring person should not be used as a reason to continue to excuse whining or untenable behavior. Nitpicking and petty criticisms, again, are simply the tools at the quickest disposal of a discontented individual who is hell bent on blaming others for that for which they should be responsible. Hiding behind compassion, if it is used to continually excuse, is a poor choice for those who want to live in truth.

Leaders must empower themselves and those they lead to see if energy is being wasted on ones who don't want to change. Desire for change is evidenced quickly from those who yearn for improvement. Change may be considered, but never or very, very slowly comes about in those who are content to work in mediocrity or lethargy. A leader who wants the success of a failing or falling employee may look for any indication of even the tiniest successes upon which to build and encourage and, in desperation, even invent them out of a struggling employee's surface appearance of effort, to try to redeem and restore. But it doesn't work where desire for change is not present, where it is not born of the content of good character. Wasted energy results from trying to solve problems for a person who doesn't want to change. So, don't expend valuable resources beyond a reasonable expectation in dealing with grievance or dysfunction where nitpicking and petty criticisms have developed their own history. Again, the costs are likely too great for the hoped for results.

The leader and the team must come to the conclusion quickly: the employee who does not want to be part of progress—rather, who wants to inhibit it—will repeatedly demonstrate signs of disconnect. The leader and others in the group need merely read the signs, and start reading them sooner as opposed to later. A lot of grief will be spared, and a lot of useful energy retained.

Worthless Consequences

Much ado about nothing is the consequence of the nitpicker, about to be borne along on the wings of excuses of failure or tolerated within a fear of fallout, and the petty criticizer, who places demands on others that he or she consistently fails to perform, who lives in destitution's double standard. Putting up with these unbridled and even intentional destructive habits is abhorrent to the leader and the group who want to live far above worthless efforts, those that produce nothing of significance.

Seeing what has been achieved, or not, in a repeating pattern is one of the surest ways to ascertain whether the person who is under-performing is costing more than his or her contributions are worth. Evaluate the results. Weigh them carefully. If they are not adding value to a project or a product, or to the people that are your producers, consider the source and develop a course of investigation as to the worth of the contributions coming out of decisions based on the faulty characters of those who drag others down.

Value-added will be seen in both theoretical and touchable ways. In theory the value-added will be noticed in heightened commitments to principles: those of trust, assurance, hope, confidence, love, reliability and truth. They become touchable when they are evidenced in actions, products and quantifiable proofs. With any disconnects between what is promised and what is delivered comes the chance, if not the real possibility, that a consequence may not be worth its expenditure.

In other words, if an employee or team member demonstrates a lack of faithfulness, perpetuates excuses, willfully spreads unmitigated blame and pursues faultfinding, nitpicking and petty criticisms, you as the leader and those you lead can be fairly certain that these tendencies and actions will continually lead to consequences of unprincipled action and lack of productivity.

Therefore, it is far better to nip the nitpicking and prevent the pettiness before they gain footholds in your work environment. Be on watch! Remember the leader desires good, but is prepared for the not good, all the time.

The Closed Door

There was an element about Jarred that was captivating and intriguing—he was an exceptionally talented man who excelled in design; indeed, his architectural drawings showcased a depth of skill and excellence of perception that was way beyond the norm. For the customer's projects to which he was assigned, his initial creativity was enviable and truly inspiring. The problem was that no job was ever finished on time, and few concrete results fully materialized out of the concepts he was creating. Plus, he was a chronic complainer, usually openly blaming others for his failures, actively criticizing the work product of others if it made him look superior. Jarred was a gifted artist, true, but more than that, he was an undisciplined contributor who, because of his talent and product, had been allowed to remain in high-level creative postures and positions without coming to grips with reality and the needful expectations of appropriately following through. No one, not even his supervisor, Dennis, had been willing to confront Jarred with the real issues, because "he was an artist, and artists, you know, can be just that way." The excuse offered was that they didn't want to hurt his feelings. But most of all, they didn't want to lose him in the company. His work was just too valuable if and when it did get done.

Apparently he was so valuable with regard to product that he had become of more value than the principle of living in truth. The acceptance of growing negatives and diminishing positives created a dysfunctional atmosphere of fear around Jarred: not stepping on eggshells and enduring the whining that accompanied missed marks became the mantra of those who had to interact with him. This "allowance factor" pervaded the work place until the department supervisor told Dennis that either Jarred shaped up, or termination would follow, period. Dennis's boss was turning up the heat, and Dennis had to be the messenger of some solid truth and consequences, whether Jarred accepted them or not.

It was past due the time that the "J" problem areas had to be addressed. Everyone connected with design knew about Jarred, "The Jartist," and all had conversed or silently agreed to try to just let him have his way, or simply avoid him, because he had been too good to push too far. But Dennis couldn't buy it anymore, nor was he allowed to; the company was simply too busy to continue to mask Jarred and temporarily shelter his dysfunction from clientele. His habitual lack of commitment to completion and constant blaming was having growing adverse effects on others even beyond the design department who had become disgusted with the passes Jarred had been given for the past two years since his hiring, so pervasive were his negative impulses' effects.

The decision to deal up-front with the Jarred issues had not been reached overnight, but once delivered the atmosphere changed instantaneously. Dennis confronted the inevitable and began to demand and enforce on-time performance, built calendars of time lines and requirements, and committed to stick to them. Specific actions were to be evaluated in a pre-determined time frame, and solid commitments to correct a problem became welcome substitutes for wondering if and when a course of action was to be enforced. The frame for success or failure was completed, its application enforced, and all was accomplished in as courteous but firm a way possible.

In a conference called to specifically discuss how the problem and the resolutions Dennis was implementing were going, Dennis was asked to report on his progress with Jarred after nearly a couple of months. Unfortunately, it was not a good report. Initially when Dennis had confronted Jarred and explained to him that requirements on his output were going to be much more attuned to timing, Jarred became overtly defensive, but then softened when he said he understood and would try. But six weeks had passed and nothing substantial had changed; several new deadlines had been missed, two appointments forgotten. The dysfunction remained the norm.

Dennis had started a file on Jarred for the express purpose of keeping track of successes and failures as the requirements were laid down. That file was not looking pretty. In the reporting meeting where Dennis had to bring his superior up to speed, a decision was made to officially put Jarred on probation for 30 days. If in that time there were not marked improvements according to a mutually agreed standard, the company would be compelled to let a very talented and undisciplined man go. This termination would be hard on several levels if it were to occur. One level was that the final work product could suffer, but most felt that his product could be replaced through another good hire if it came to this. The more important consideration was that because Jarred's product was so well liked and his dysfunction had been excused so many times previously, some people could already "feel the pain" with what they were fairly certain was coming. Many believed this could become very uncomfortable.

Dennis thought about the reasons he could give Jarred for the decision-path he was having to take—and none of them were the truth except to say, in as gentle and yet forthright ways as possible, that Jarred was failing in character of aptitude and attitude, not competence of art. Indeed, Dennis rehearsed, "Jarred, if you learn it here you won't have to learn this elsewhere."

Dennis scheduled a review "come to the truth" meeting with Jarred—and it went poorly. In fact, two days later, Jarred quit, no notice given. Perhaps that resignation became a sort of convenience for the company in not having to fire him, but in this regard Jarred had lost not only his job but also an opportunity to grow in his character. He was unwilling to face hard truths he needed to face to help him mature. And he took his same problem-package into his next two jobs.

Dennis saw Jarred in a coffee bar about six months after Jarred's departure, and they talked briefly. The story would have a happy ending if it could be said that Jarred had learned and wished to develop in faithfulness. He had not, and now without work after a third termination he was beat down and again blaming everyone else for his own lack of responsibility. Dennis listened for a time, but couldn't say much—this door to providing help, truth, encouragement and direction was closed, at least for that moment and with that person.

The dysfunction in Jarred's story was occurring inside and outside his original workplace, permeating his life in other significant relationships, and then became apparent in two additional positions. Because Jarred was "officially gone" from Dennis's company, it may have been easy or at least convenient for Dennis to completely ignore the obvious when he ran into Jarred in the coffee bar. But because Dennis cared, he wanted to at least be supportive if Jarred desired this. Because Jarred didn't, Dennis couldn't, and isolation still gripped its prey.

Some would say that it was far better for the health of the company that Jarred was removed, and now that he was gone, who should care about what had happened? Those expressions would be acceptable perhaps, to a point. Continual lack of follow through, blaming, criticizing, nitpicking, fault-finding—

these negative attributes Jarred displayed affected the company no longer because they were conducted on the outside and in other venues; the resolution was huge because Jarred was gone.

But Dennis viewed this situation differently. Even though he realized the obvious, that Jarred and his work product were no longer his responsibility, he was also a man who wanted others to win, even someone as difficult as Jarred. Dennis believed that if anyone desired to learn from past mistakes and sought to become better regardless of location or position, it would or could be profitable to help if help was requested and accepted. If Dennis could have invested to a point where Jarred convinced himself to cease his complaining and mature, there may have been hope for a win. However, since it didn't happen, the whining with its destructive influences remained.

The poignant reality is this: if Dennis had tried when the door remained fastened shut, he would have wasted his energy and nothing would have come from the effort—except a worthless consequence. Dennis made a good decision in walking away and not chasing Jarred. Jarred was not to be reached, and this by his own choice. In fact, it had taken too long to determine this unfortunate truth, and a lot of energy had been wasted as faultfinding continued unabated.

These three—wanton faultfinding, wasted energy and worthless consequences—drain a leader's creative energy and a group's solution perspectives if allowed to grow unchecked. To create industrial strength solutions, the negatives, when they appear, are to be confronted within an atmosphere of constructive teaching and corrective action. If, in the course of confrontation, the person who represents the sources of the dysfunctions owns them, turns from them, and replaces them with positive desires for improvement, then the win is multiple within many lives and stages of productivity. Clearly with victories like this a stage is set for the many benefits of working the workable solutions.

Chapter 4:
Mixing and Matching—
Work the Workable Solutions

Lincoln letter to J. M. Brockman, Esq.

After Abraham Lincoln had reached prominence as a lawyer and politician, he received a note from a John M. Brockman, dated September 24th, 1860, asking Mr. Lincoln the processes of acquiring knowledge of the legal profession. Lincoln's answer of September 25th is intriguing and tells us much about his beliefs regarding the value of work.

J. M. Brockman, Esq.

Dear Sir: Yours of the 24th asking "the best mode of obtaining a thorough knowledge of the law" is received. The mode is very simple, though laborious, and tedious. It is only to get the books, and read, and study them carefully…Work, work, work, is the main thing.

Yours very truly,

A. Lincoln

What is work anyway, especially since, according to Mr. Lincoln, it is the main thing? And how does one's work relate to what has become known as a work ethic?

Work, as we understand and deal with it today, is at least this: the tangible efforts one exercises to achieve a desired result, usually accompanied by rewards of commensurate value. Whether you are the employer or the employee, retired or just beginning your career, engaged as a student or the teacher, sufficient in wealth or living paycheck to paycheck, you work. You work if you agree with the definition above. And while work isn't optional, the attitudes that accompany it certainly are.

Compare work to a work ethic. "Work ethic" is a value-sensitive and value-inclusive term. The definition of "work ethic" carries a value perspective as a moral good, and includes degrees of decision-making as to the importance one places on his or her work and his or her honest recognition and acceptance to act responsibly to uphold and fulfill duty well.

Ask a cross-section of people what determines the quality of an individual's work ethic and you may receive scores of different responses. Factors included in the answer as to cause and effect may include demographics, socio-economic levels, upbringing, age, health, experience, education, environment, success of parents or guardians, national and world economy, country of origin, citizenship, culture, ethnicity, personality, worldview, religion, beliefs about government, responsibility, fate, chance, and change. You may also hear responses from viewpoints of optimism, pessimism, complacency, commitment, determination, or defeat. Season of life may come into play, too, as might luck, encouragement, discouragement and hope.

All the reference points are important and all are factors to a degree. In the first three chapters you read about the work ethic determiner called "desire." People express desire. Then they decide. And their decisions are influenced by much of the above, and much of the above is influenced by the decisions of maturing people. It's almost a "chicken-egg" discussion as to origin, but maybe not quite.

I have an elderly mother, approaching 90 years of age, who is in exceptional health not only for this stage of life, but in general, for which we are grateful. Her active lifestyle and desire to maintain if not grow it, along with years of healthy eating and good life-style habits combine to contribute to her longevity and alertness, as does her forward focus—of this I am confident. She would say she is "blessed" and I agree with that, too. Sure, she has her days of discomfort, sometimes severe, when the arthritis flares up and the irritation and frustration of an aging body, along with the joints that hurt and movements that are slow, make it tough for her to function as she desires. It is amazing to observe the differences in perspective and outlook, as they relate to physical pain or the lack of it, in her or anyone else, present company included. Yes, you and I are subject to the same; when we feel well and healthy we may look at our worlds differently than when we are ill. A balanced life perception tells us that this ebb and flow is part of the human condition. Some would call it "normal."

So let's take this a step further. When "how I feel" is applied to work environments where certain legal, time-sensitive, project-related, money-driven, goal-achievable, numbers-pushed and customer-demanded outcomes become motivators, the reasons or excuses some express because of discomfiture, regardless of the source, are weighed more carefully to see what their true importance is, and whether or not causes for "missing work" are acceptable and right.

Work ethic comes into play when a decision is made whether to be present and accounted for, productive and rewarded for doing so, or not, and often this decision and its motives provide a true test of character at the most elementary levels. For example, one who uses "sick days" as false reasons for exiting or being absent needs to understand what they are doing: they are lying. "Floating days" or "employee option" days are terms that should be used more often where agreement as to a need for flexibility exists. But if you are not sick, don't say you are. Using a day designated for illness and recuperation for some other reason is a violation of integrity. By the way, that important "I" word—standing for Integrity, takes center stage shortly.

There is a difference between a work ethic and work ethics. The term "work ethics" is defined as a collection of behavioral styles or habits that constitute observable efforts to achieve desired outcomes. Here's the difference and inter-working relationship between the terms:

- A work ethic reflects moral standing.
- Work ethics are the actions that produce the products coming from right decisions to employ good morals.

Given these definitions it may be concluded that, in growing industrial strength solutions, strong and productive work ethics constitute the actions that prove a work ethic's principled good. Its moral foundations are as follows: integrity, decision-making, commitment, and faithfulness to duty. These four attributes become four standards that a leader or organization uses to fashion its workable solutions.

The mixtures of people, who are, in the final analysis, the Workable Solutions, are made up of their educations, experiences and environments, and it is they who become strong solution-providers when they agree on the four standards. Their creative mixtures empower effective task completion and produce most desired results. Working the Workable Solutions means fully engaging the people who are the ones who give meaning and momentum to accomplishing their jobs well. These are the people whose work ethic empowers their work ethics. When empowered, the benefits obtained from their individual and collective efforts are far-reaching.

A close examination of The Four Standards reveals the satisfaction that comes from their consistent application.

Industrial strength solutions, to be most effective, must include them.

The Four Standards

The four standards are the ingredients that make workable solutions strong. These really are to be seen as a continuum, unbroken and sequential, building upon one another.

First, <u>Integrity</u>: So many interpretations exist within the understandings of this word, so for clarity let's make it simpler: integrity is the quest for truth and the expression of it. At the center of an individual that person's integrity, or its lack thereof, becomes a pivot point upon which character rests and decisions are made. Truth is revealed as facts become known and honest treatments of those facts become the actions that say whether or not integrity is being applied into life. People working together, if they do it well, have to take basic stock of their truthfulness, and upon that reality, decide their levels of trust and cooperation stemming from the degree of their commitment to integrity.

Second, <u>Decision-making</u>: We all make decisions moment by moment. Some are clearly more monumental than others. Decisions matter. Choices count. Over the long haul the collection of small decisions and the necessity of epic ones take prominent roles in fashioning a life. Decisions are born of desire, and for them to be good and able to produce good things, they must be based on integrity (discovered and applied truth). It is then that decisions are ready to stand up to the tests of invasive negative circumstances. A person who decides is a person who moves toward setting courses and committing to their fulfillment when what has been decided is based on knowledge and is focused on creating benefits.

Third, <u>Commitment</u>: More than a decision, it is the applied follow-up to cause a decision to become action toward fulfillment of a purpose. There's an endurance factor with commitment that elevates it above temporal setbacks, inconveniences, or just plain difficult barriers that have to be crossed or destroyed in order to complete the objectives. Commitment is the force that puts actions to words. Commitment is the child of Integrity and good Decision-making when the person who has honestly decided on his or her course becomes unsatisfied until the action commences, the end is in view, and the prize is won.

Fourth, <u>Faithfulness to Duty</u>: Faithfulness is the proof that commitment is working because results are ever in sight: jobs get done within an agreed time line or ahead of time, goals are reached or exceeded, tasks and details are fulfilled, communication loops are closed, there are no "dangling participles" of ineffectiveness where someone has "dropped the ball" or doesn't own accountability or is not dependable. Faithfulness to duty says that obligation is fulfilled and that the finish is not only done, it is done well.

These four standards are the ingredients of Workable Solutions—they are the standards that drive the people who make the solutions work, and create industrial strength. These are the foundations to successful solutions to business challenges and they work every time they are employed fully. They are the ethics behind the work.

For the greatest resilience to be achieved, matching people's strengths appropriately with differing aspects of accomplishing a goal is just plain smart. It is appropriate and right to place strengths where they are needed most. Purposeful matching and proper aligning include a holistic approach to solving problems or fulfilling tasks, and when accomplished within high ethics, complete the people in the outworking of the processes.

Far from stirring up unhealthy competition, the exercise of matching talents, gifts, abilities, and capabilities to achieve mutual support and success in the accomplishment of a project makes good sense. Where one person is the larger vision person, another can take the global picture and break it down into doable parts. Another person who possesses administrative strengths creates calendars of action and accountability while others handle finances, move product, take care of correspondence and answer phones. You get the idea.

There is nothing unusual here in an appropriate division of responsibilities, except that founded on The Four Standards, the Workable Solutions cooperate with one another, are cohesive and connected. Collective endeavors are engaged within their own mixtures, free of needless encumbrances like dishonesty, weak excuses, distrust, lying and indecisiveness, laziness, giving up, or cashing out. The reason workable solutions work is simple to state although sometimes hard to achieve: everyone shares the values of the standards, the responsibilities of achievement, and all should share in the rewards.

Some people call the collection of people who labor together a team, a work group, a band, an assembly, a unit, a cluster, a division, a board, a department, an organization, an assemblage or a congregation. No matter the term, the meaning's essence is this: these are people joined by a bond of values and responsibility—their premises are unified, their roles understood, their expectations reasonable, their results predictable and their rewards sure.

The Four Standards
The Constitution of Workable Solutions

Integrity	Decision-Making	Commitment	Faithfulness
The quest and expression of truth	The choices you make that count	The point where decisions become actions	The proof of when duty is fulfilled well

Work ethic is the moral foundation; work ethics are the actions that show agreement with, and the follow-through upon, the values inherent in the foundation. People who join together to accomplish a task form the workable solutions that a leader and organization desire. The four standards are the ingredients that make the cooperative mixture of people match strengths to needs.

Everyone in a group, regardless of size, bears responsibility and ownership to see that workable solutions are given life, nourished, and activated. Far from being a lesson in chemistry, responsibility is a state of being and doing where lessons of character are born again of desire and seen in responsible activity. Indeed, the solutions — the combinations of people and how they work together to achieve mutual goals — are the direct products of what they desire. What we want is what we get.

A structure is needed in which workable solutions can be given life, survive and thrive. At Creative Team Resources Group, Inc. (www.ctrg.com) we provide such a structure. We call it a Core Team.

The Core Team

A core team is a structure, and it is much more. A core team is a living and breathing entity made up of people who are committed to certain unalterable truths. It is a workable solution, a group who practices commitment to truths in daily activity — at home, at work, school, wherever they are. A core team is founded on these essential premises: people are more important than production and relationships precede and give definition to function. Or, put another way, the "who" of this workable solution comes before and gives birth to the "do" of the team.

Relationships are primary and are defined as the decisions a team member makes in support of another team member's success. Function is defined as the observable actions that prove the validity of the decisions. When people know and are convinced that they are more important than what they do, they cause the value of what they do to increase because they show that their product is a true representation of the quality of their decisions.

A core team promotes and demonstrates the truth of its premise, and does so through its structure and commensurate activity. A core team is known by the descriptions inherent in its name, describing its character and contribution. Here's the breakout:

C: The "C" of Core stands for Consistency. Authenticity is best seen when people do what they say they are going to do, where faithfulness and commitment are primary attributes of a working relationship, or any relationship for that matter, and the people are authentically accountable in recurring episodes, constituting literally a pattern of proof.

O: The "O" of Core represents Obedience. The obedience described here is agreement and willful choice to adhere to and act upon agreed and shared core values, those attributes of intangible yet firmly planted principles that form the basis of decisions and desires.

R: The "R" signifies Relationships, a term which has already been described as the decisions by one team member to support another team member's success. In this definition the relationships are seen as right, strong and good, and promote and sustain workable solutions.

E: The "E" stands for Example. As we often say in our consulting training classes, the issue is not whether a person has an example; the issue is what kind of example he or she has. All people on a Core Team are exemplary; they choose the kind of good or bad examples they will model to those who serve with them and to those who observe their results.

T: The "T" denotes Trust. There is no team in great form and producing exemplary function without trust present and openly demonstrated. Indeed a healthy and growing relationship cannot exist without it, trust is a part of its very core essence, and as functional contributions are motivated by it, it becomes a driving force for excellence. Trust is unearned as relationships begin and is earned through its functions, growing over time, as merits are proven and relationships deepen.

E: The "E" of Team stands for the Essentials of a person's composite nature. People are complicated mixtures and structures in and of themselves; each person comes with unique sets of experience, education, and environment that contribute to individuality and, within a group, welcomed and needful diversity. Experience, education and environment to a large degree are chosen for a child, but adults choose these three essentials every time they come to work, making those choices and the reasons behind them fundamentally important.

A: The "A" represents Accountability. Authenticity of character and contribution is impossible without accountability. Assurance seen in faithfulness and reliability is a product of the choice to be accountable. Any team who chooses accountability will create an atmosphere of personal as well as group responsibility where each member strives for multiple connection points between relationships and functions, and frankly are not satisfied until function and relationship are illustrative of each other on a consistent basis. Further, a leader demonstrates accountability to the team before ever requiring accountability from its membership; indeed that leader's model provides the impetus for shared accountability that each person initiates, deciding to hold him or her self accountable before seeking it from another.

M: The "M" represents Method, defined as what work is made of, how it is accomplished and rewarded. Method includes desire, decision and drive for excellence in task accomplishment, the insatiable yearning to always find a better way, utilizing personal, organizational, personnel, and materiel resources well, and then improving on our improvements.

The structure and operational efficiencies of a core team are those where the relationships—the decisions for consistency, obedience to shared values, right choices about team member's successes, chosen examples, trust (unearned and earned), essentials of uniqueness of each person's person and production— constitute primary and initial incentives in paving the path to functions. Functions are the methods that work well because the people have made their relationships work first. The letters of "Core" and "Team" are in spelling and sequential order of importance and application. Representations of relationships and functions on a core team are evidences of solid work ethic seen in contributory work ethics. It's a marriage in ideals and in deeds. The team is wise that often reviews and renews these words and what they represent.

Core team members embrace values agreement. What is not expected: that all core team participants will share identical personal values. What is expected and upon which strong foundations are built: that all core team members agree on the essential values of their team.

Core Team and Personal Values Intersection Points

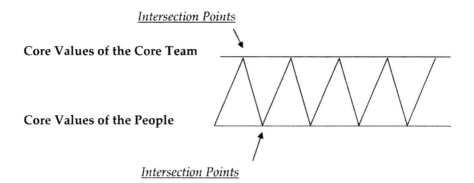

Great strength results where the values of the individuals intersect with the core values of the team, as the chart above illustrates. This grid is strong because of its points of interconnectivity. Sever one or more, and the resulting severe disconnect would be detrimental to relationships and functions, potentially affecting the integrity of the entire structure and its operation.

A core team who is relationally strong in its values, including consistency, obedience, relationships, examples, trust, who understands and appreciates its essentials of composite nature, and who seeks to be authentically accountable, is in the best position to accomplish its methods well. Because the members are healthy they seek to un-complicate their methods, involve more people, and give them the tools they need to accomplish their roles. Actions like these demonstrate trust at a level that encourages participants to produce greater value, value-added, and therefore more viable and necessary options—evidences of the workable solutions.

Methods not only include actions—they also incorporate proper utilization of the resources that make the actions possible. In healthy organizations there is a high degree of dedication to proper stewardship (the responsibility-driven care in the acquisition and management of value-items entrusted to a worker or team member's oversight) of that organization's resources. The degree of stewardship seen from core team members in action is a direct indicator of how much worth is shared within and from the people with regard to the company's assets.

A "Resource Needs Assessment" (RNA) is a tool that can be used to assess the inventory, care (stewardship) and need for acquisition of resources essential to solid productivity, and it is included as an appendix to *Industrial Strength Solutions*. The RNA looks carefully at three broad categories of resources: personnel, materiel, and time. The *Industrial Strength Solutions* model of proper resource treatment and implementation encourages balance in people and their production and showcases the importance of workable solutions that can contribute well because they are provisioned well. Workers without the right tools may have great motives and fail in their methods. Appropriate, regular, and enhanced training is encouraged for people who want to develop, in current as well as broadening areas of engagement on a core team. Businesses that seek new heights of achievement in product development, service provision, customer satisfaction, and their own people's development, look for creative training opportunities.

You are encouraged to view and utilize the RNA, found on page 213. Permission is granted for photocopying the document, altering it to your specifications, and using it within your environment and applications. If photocopied, please state the following: "Used with permission of Creative Team Resources Group, Inc. (CTRG), www.ctrg.com."

As referenced above, the third resource in addition to personnel and materiel is time. Let's highlight its importance here. No one is given more time in a day than anyone else, and it is a resource with no guarantees that it will be able to be used tomorrow. Therefore, it is important that we dwell on this vital topic before moving from the constitution of what makes up a successful core team.

How Important is Time Management on a Core Team?

Included among the many appreciable resources that core teams possess and utilize, as part of their daily methodology, is this asset of time. The consideration is not whether it is used, but how well. As a team grows to understand the values of its participants and their contributions, the evidence mounts that one of the most blatant indicators of effectiveness, or lack thereof, is how a group utilizes this most precious of resources, one that when it is consumed is gone forever; and, even more importantly, why a team chooses to consume it in the fashions they employ.

Inefficient time management should not be considered an indigenous condition in a group's make up, it is not imposed because of tradition or habit ("We've always done 'it' this way!"), even though the forces are strong that encourage repetitive routine as an only child. As part of a method of work, appropriate time utilization must deliberately and regularly be chosen as to its implementation in every team member's consistent routine, common regimen, encompassing all work decisions and activities, every day.

To use time wisely in a productive environment, a workable solution of individuals will recognize and weigh the circumstances over which it has no control, while exercising deliberate decisions regarding those conditions over which it does have governance and responsibility, consisting of these pro-active choices:

1.   How the team will respond to unanticipated or uninvited changes, those imposed modifications that every business faces, because the group wants to treat their resources and the people who use them with respect, and…

2.   Understanding that superior time utilization is an investment that produces quantitative as well as qualitative rewards, not altered in character nor consumed in exercise by the impending or present changes; rather, where the character of the group is seen through its effective use of time, helping the necessary changes succeed and even excel beyond their expectations.

The Commitment

Mary Ann is a chief administrator, working for a non-profit entity, supervising three other administrators. She is a good leader of people, eager to learn and apply lessons of management effectiveness, and not unwilling to challenge the status quo in her quests for better methods if she deems them needful. In advance of an email interview granted to me as part of the preparation of this book, she polled her people to see what behavioral changes they would be willing to make to better utilize their time more efficiently and accountably and provide superior service to the staff they support. Their results are to be seen below.

But before viewing and weighing their perspectives, we must consider this: one characteristic often observed of the inner-workings of a non-profit organization consists of the degrees of unassigned time, the allocation of which depends on staff members' prerogatives, producing a whole lot of granted or implied freedom which paid team members are to utilize to get their jobs done. This freedom can be tied to the need to motivate and train a non-profit organization's volunteers, encouraging them toward measurable and increased productivity that in most non-profit environments usually originates from high passion for its cause. In healthy non-profit organizations, freedom of time and function, in cooperation, constitute marks of provisional strength and engaged fulfillment for which the organization was initially formed.

However, one of the great temptations of freedom of time and function in a non-profit environment, if not monitored closely, and if ownership of responsibility is not applied diligently, is that time literally can be thrown away on accomplishing non-essentials, discarded on worthless chores, simply wasted and tossed as would be the garbage on Thursday, therefore spoiling not only the resources of staff, but in essence and perhaps directly, pillaging contributor's funds right along side. When this condition becomes known, and it is articulated and confronted with a view toward correction and more accountability, it may often be excused on the basis of what is perceived to be lower expectations of team or individual contributions, because, well, "This organization isn't run like a business."

Does that assessment ever rankle me! If running a non-profit entity "like a business," in alignment and agreement with proper and good value systems, means that its adherents follow the admonitions and prerequisites of a for-profit enterprise whose stake-holders have an expectation of high productivity, and who, because of their investment demand more, should the contributors of charitable funds require any less in an organization that ostensibly exists to perform good deeds on behalf of higher causes, and even expect and command additional output because the cause is greater? The answer is this: the expectations of the for-profit should be exceeded by the expectations of the non-profit from performers and stake-holders because the standards of committed and passionate people, if targeted and utilized well, should, and always will, out-perform duties of contribution in organizations where a paycheck is offered as sole compensation to workers who care only about what they get, and for which money may be the only motive for their involvements.

Earnest motivation from passion gives life and enduring enthusiasm to expanded contributions from committed people if they are dedicated to the organization's cause, whether they are paid or volunteer their time and energy. A non-profit has just as much if not more reason and motivation for excellence than a for-profit may have. Where commitment is high for the right reasons from the right people, more can be acquired and literally required from volunteers who are appreciated for their value and the values of their contributions. The measuring tool of the committed volunteer is not compensation in terms of coin, of course; rather, compensation in terms of cause, motivated and completed by character.

Whether the challenge of a non-profit is to run it more "like a business" or, regardless of its label, in a way that fulfills its duties with high accountability based on enduring principle, then we should expect and require enhanced positive decisions regarding appropriate and contributory utilization of resources, one of which is the single-use element of time. Once consumed it is forever departed unless in its consumption it has produced products that live and endure in importance "beyond time."

"It is time for time to be used well." This is a sentence that should be on the break-room refrigerator of every enterprise, posted in every factory, in every boardroom, at every desk, at every job site. Mary Ann and her team, in their non-profit enterprise, believe in and seek to practice this maxim. Again, they were asked what behavioral changes they would employ to save time for their leaders as well as themselves, to increase their efficiency factors, raise their accountability and provide enhanced service. Combining their answers as to methods, here is Mary Ann's Core Team list:

1. Communicate effectively, assuring that communication is completed the first time, listen well and appropriately respond by asking important questions, in order to cut down needs for returning to original sources for clarification that should already be present.

2. Take initiative to discover what items or issues are vitally important, including those that are time sensitive, and prioritize your own work based on these criteria, instead of first asking a supervisor to do so. Change the priorities willingly if the need to change is induced or required by your superior.

3. Organize your work, and keep it organized. Sloppiness contributes only to confusion and lack of attention to prioritization.

4. Accomplish specific tasks in assigned time blocks, such as budget analysis, funds disbursements, collections, AR and AP.

5. Limit opportunities for interruptions, set boundaries to prevent unnecessary requests by closing the office door if needed to assure fulfillment of a prioritized task.

6. Adopt an attitude and resulting action of proactive focus, anticipating before reacting.

7. Research independently, before you ask for help.

8. Create lists of tasks and take notes at meetings to ensure compliance and conclusive action steps.

9. Check your work for errors and make corrections before the work is handed in. Submit the required and completed assignments in full, not sections or disjointedly, to limit needs for interruptions for further clarification.
10. Come to work with a pro-active and service-directed attitude.
11. Exercise flexibility when inevitable changes occur.
12. Help each member of the team understand his or her tasks fully.

This is a core team composed of industrial strength solution providers. Well done! You can imagine the positive outcomes this group regularly contributes to its non-profit organization. These folks represent stellar examples of faithfulness and eagerness of accomplishment of tasks (function), while supporting each other's successes (relationship), raising their own bars of methodological excellence to provide models of increasingly efficient uses of time, one of their most cherished resources. Those who are the recipients of the work of this team are well-inspired to pursue paths of similar accomplishment in their paid positions, and volunteers who interact with this administrative group are shown true methods of passionately engaging in an enterprise because of the cause, motivated by good characters, money notwithstanding.

Time management is part of a greater standard of utilizing well the resources entrusted to the team, whether in a for-profit or non-profit organization. Great time management consists of deliberate choices that committed core team members make in their work practice every day. Time management is not a condition inherent in the rote punching of a clock; rather, its effective use is seen as a demonstration of adherence to good character and high values in productive atmospheres where constant choices to "do it better" permeate the mix of people who engage to create better results.

The term, "Core Team," represents its constitution and level of commitment. While the name designation of your group may be different, you have a Core Team if you have a cluster where the solution—the mix that constitutes your particular assemblage—is founded on certain immovable principles that all participants agree are right, and who acts upon them with all their might. The commitment level to the strength of the relationships overcomes the challenges of "wrong mixes" or "combinations of difficult personalities" because decisions of how working relationships work—the choices based on desires and values agreement—are primary in importance and functionality, and are therefore unalterable, a clear demonstration of a solid work ethic.

It is from this mix of proper motive that motivation comes to acquire, invent, maintain, care for, increase the value of, and properly engage with the right tools, the provisioned materiel that the team needs to do its functions with excellence. Watch and appreciate how a team uniquely birthed from core values is unwaveringly committed to properly valuing its tools. A condition of strong relationships committed to solid methods represents a mix of characteristics that are tied inseparably to each other. This mix works in cooperative concert to achieve solid and growing product provision through maturing individuals.

Workable Solutions form the Core Team and cause the group to work together well. Build one, and see if the solutions work for you. Recognize that solutions that bear success are those that have the best interests of the people involved as primary. Working the workable solutions, based on what we really want, is possible when the complement of the Core Team mix is recognized for the worth of its people first, before the team engages in its provision.

The Core Team
A Functioning Workable Solution

C: Consistency
O: Obedience to shared values
R: Relationships
E: Example

T: Trust
E: Essentials of Composite Nature
A: Accountability
M: Method

The Blend

The art of blending good mixtures to obtain positive outcomes is practiced in many areas of application and operation: teams, chemistry, coffee drinks, culinary art, diverse cultures, cosmetics, colors, the perfect margarita, newlyweds, compost, smoothies, fuel additives, singers, paints, and even sound. And speaking of sound, today with more advanced technology and more sophisticated recording and production equipment, the human ear is rarely satisfied with mediocrity or yesterday's mix when it comes to great audio. I know one man who should know.

Larry is the consummate professional sound technician in the studio and for the live concert stage. Whenever I have had the opportunity as a stage performer to entrust the audio of my presentation to Larry, I am always at ease. In fact, for readers who are familiar with the intricacies of stage presentations and their dependence on the interface with audio and technical support, you will appreciate that in 25 years of working with Larry he has *never once* given me a dead mike.

In his interview for *Industrial Strength Solutions*, I posed 7 questions for his consideration. Larry's answers revealed much about mixing sound, and by extension, blending people on teams to create great core groups, organizational units, who, in their character, represent and produce quality industrial strength solutions in much the same ways Larry produces great sound. The similarities are striking.

Questions and Answers:

1. *What is the process technically you go through to achieve great sound?*
Larry answered that first and foremost you must know the room in which you are working, and then match sound and type of music to that specific environment. Understand the environment and then combine the elements, utilizing the people who have the capability to make it all work together well. Further, a thorough knowledge of your gear (your tools) allows the flexibility to produce the end result required, whether you are producing rock and roll, jazz, "easy-listening," or anything else. By knowing how to combine what is needed, you stand the best chance to achieve what you want.
This application is not difficult. Great teams are formed in cooperative and creative environments where agreement exists on principles and practices to produce desired results. To right environments add the elements of the people and their materiel that are combined to work together to provide solid solutions and excellent products. The variety of the products may exceed initial limits as people's creativity is unleashed and encouraged. This environment exists to support the quality its people bring to the opportunity.

2. *What are some of the hardest challenges to achieving what you want?*
The items on Larry's list were at first surprising. They were

environment, equipment, and people. Interesting, isn't it, that these are the same items needed for a great technical process to produce a great artistic result? Further, Larry explained that, in this context, environment consists of areas outside, inside, large, small, and reflective vs. non-reflective surfaces, heights, corners; all of these are matters of containment as to how much and what kinds of audio will be required to fill a room. I asked Larry, "How is sound to be contained?" Larry said, "Through your equipment, and knowing how to use it well, realizing that overkill kills and distorts the product; under-utilization strains the ear. The basic rule is this: when the system is being worked at full capacity, only 50% is being used." Finally, I asked, "What parts do the people play?" I thought his answer was most intriguing. People are the best gauges. Larry said, "Sound is subjective, an art and not a science. There is always a contestant that can do the job 'better' in his or her opinion. The arts breed ego; handling ego is part of mixing well." Wow.

Here are the salient points we will extract. First, the choice of an environment in which a core team will contribute is vital to the freedom and creative impetus the team will enjoy in engaging their efforts. Treated as an essential it contributes the structure into which solutions can be molded. Environment is a structure that allows freedom.

Second, tools of the trade, materiel required to start and complete a job, must be handled well, through people who care as much about the equipment as they do the products they are making.

Finally for this question, teamwork, like sound, is subjective, an art and not a science. While a great painting will yearn for a frame that enhances its beauty and draws the eye, we must remember that the painting is not the frame, and the frame is not the painting. One serves the other, and this truth should characterize the cooperation on a core team that functions within a structure that promotes its members as well as enhances and encourages their contributions. There is no room here for run-away egos in a group that engages in structured art; rather, cooperation reigns and these people exercise self-control.

3. *What is your motive in creating good sound?*

Larry's answer focused on the goal of provision: serving the customer. "Ultimately the audience needs to enjoy the presentation and leave with the passion for it that I have. Therefore, a good night for me is when what I do becomes 'invisible' as to the effects. People know that they had a great time, heard a great concert, and were not focused on why it was good; rather, that it just was good. The goal for me is effective and enduring communication of passion and meaning." What a terrific answer.

Our extrapolation is this: the goal of a team is best fulfilled in qualitative service to those who receive (consume) the products the team produces. The process to the end-user may not, and, likely could not, include a full knowledge of the elements that contributed to the excellence the customer enjoys. However, the industrial strength solution group who works together well knows that the methods used to produce great products include recognizing and building people of passion who, through their respective contributions and cooperative efforts, share that passion freely, and it is this result that a consumer accurately interprets as excellence.

4. *How do you know you have achieved success?*

Larry explained that when great performances occur, and sound has been one vital element in the accomplishment of that success, several people are pleased. They include the artists, tour managers, friends or acquaintances of the artists, as well as the audience in general who probably paid for the privilege. He also noted that, conversely, if complaining occurs from any of these sources because technical mistakes interrupt the flow of the message or the artistic moments the performers have rehearsed and diligently prepared, the bottom line is that the message is apt to be lost. All serious artists, and certainly those for whom Larry works, care greatly about their message, that it appropriately, without disturbance or distraction, reaches and touches their audiences with meaning.

We can learn an important truth here, and it is this: in a working environment when forthright, pro-active and proper concentration and energy are expended on solving problems because a core team cares more about ultimate success on behalf of the end-user than it does trying to avoid failure or cast blame if mistakes do occur, that team raises its chances of achieving satisfaction, providing "meaning" for the customer, simply because the contributors desire to live and contribute toward the good instead of fostering the failure and blame that comes from inadequate or ineffective planning and execution. Proactive solutions often remove problems that should be outside the realm of control or concern of the people who are to enjoy the result of a team's provision. Further, when quality comes as a result of a team's dedicated efforts, its "audience" will be pleased and will let their producers know through compliments, additional sales, and requests for "more." It is always good to leave an audience desiring "more" because what they received met or exceeded their initial expectations.

5. Why is blending important?

Larry composed an illustration. "Taking a group of instrumentalists on their own, having all of these musicians play simultaneously at different levels, gives the listener fatigue..." (I'll say, and, among other things, includes monster frustration) "...in trying to figure out which instruments are leading, or which structure is providing a focus point. Is it rhythm, lead lines, fills, vocals? Therefore, blending is needed to put all the instruments, as they are being played, into their proper places in the listening environment, to bring together what the artist intends in the first place."

Larry is at home in a recording studio, of course, but his passion is as a producer of live audio where often the demands of mixing are not framed by controlled environments that the studio provides. Bottom line—it is more difficult outside than inside. The outside audience is often more demanding because they want the product in that venue to "sound like the recording." Therefore Larry's job is to exceed expectations that the outside environment could otherwise dictate so his customers receive a comfort level of provision that contributes to total reception of the message. Larry's job is to assure, as much as he can, that the recipient doesn't have to work for that which he or she purchased in the first place.

The applications here are varied and vital. First, blending great contributors as well as their contributions makes the whole a lot more satisfying to the buyer. Some contributions will be more "out in front" than others and in a healthy environment of industrial strength solutions, no one will care who gets the credit; all contribute to the success, regardless of who is heard or seen in the end.

Second, the environment should not control; it is to be controlled and thereby become a contributor to a successful venture of provision, even if the demands in producing quality are increased because they have to overcome obstacles. An end-user should be pleased, period, because the provider has done the job well, no matter what.

6. *How difficult is it to train others to do what you do?*

Larry stated that there are several factors when looking at a prospective associate. First, the question is asked: does the apprentice have a basic ability to play an instrument or perform with his or her voice as an instrument, regardless of the level of experience they may have amassed so far, and does the applicant have a basic understanding of an instrument's capability and placement, or the composition and capability of the human voice? The reasons behind these criteria are that the person who runs the sound must comprehend and therefore relate to the unique requirements of the execution of the task.

A second question is this: does the candidate possess a passion for doing what audio engineering requires, a drive to communicate through good sound? Larry expounded, "Passion is seen when the audio engineer shows a true desire to make excellence happen, he or she is not just filling a space, is not trying to attract attention or glamour that may accompany that position or job. When a prospective candidate for audio engineering comes before me, these factors become lessons that are covered over a period of time as mentoring and apprenticeship takes place."

A third element is attitude. Said Larry, "It is easy to let ego get caught up because of the money and the professional equipment involved, and the audio engineer is the driver in this car on a power trip in more ways than one. But egotistic attitudes have no place in a service dedicated to blending well. Sometimes, because quality is required consistently, the ego can't stand repetition, and ego becomes less of a factor long-term." Ego comes to naught when it prevents relationships from maturing and a better product developing. "What is more important: quality of work, or character? In the end, character wins."

Larry's bullets, as applicable to core teams, are these: is there a basic understanding of roles and responsibilities that accompany a person's desire to participate on the team? Next, does a prospective member showcase genuine passion for the hard work that his or her provision will require? Third, what kind of attitude of service does the new member bring in support of the goal and support of the whole? There is no place for egos run amuck in the cooperative workings of a team that wants and needs to blend their efforts to achieve greatness. In fact, greatness will refine and ultimately subjugate misplaced ego if the ego-centered person truly wants to remain on a team whose members base their actions on right motives, and engage in right methods, for the right results.

7. Finally, when it all "works," how does it make you feel?

Larry explained that in taking a large stage set-up with many musicians, at times including a full orchestra, positioning and blending them well, seeing the artist walk on stage and begin to sing, in that moment, to feel the dynamics of the evening along with great artistry, "…can on a really good night drive me to the point of tears, a pure emotional connection when communication is taking place at a level that can only be achieved when the mix and message are right and tight."

In Larry's audio world this happens a lot and represents a recurring reward for his conscientious efforts at blending the right elements in the right way. In fulfilling his responsible functions to blend and mix sound well, efforts toward excellence are not optional. When all the factors of equipment, room, people, and egos are considered, "…you have to remember that what you are doing is communicating. Communication is the goal…therefore use the elements wisely and mix them well."

This is the chronicle not only of a professional audio technician, but also of a competent, caring, and cooperative core team that works in concert with its values, and contributes wealth through its health.

The commitment level to the strength of the relationships overcomes the challenges of "wrong mixes" or "combinations of difficult personalities" because decisions of how working relationships work—the choices based on desires and values agreement—are primary in importance and functionality, and are therefore unalterable, a clear demonstration of a solid work ethic.

The Turnabout

Core teams work well when they demonstrate strong relationships in positive and declared decisions members make about each other's successes. Support comes in many ways, but always is initiated from the people who want to make a difference.

Jo Ann is a Senior Accountant in a government agency. Her story is a captivating one. When the Core Team concept was first presented to her department, various degrees of appreciation and apprehension were evidenced throughout the group of nearly 120 people. Over the course of time, actually several months, certain fundamental truths began to send their roots deep into the soil of what was becoming fertile ground in the planting of strong relationships, and what kind of results Jo Ann's department could and should expect when the plants began to flower.

The day of "The Turnabout" came almost unexpectedly to the CTRG consultant on site. In a regular reinforcement meeting with Jo Ann, she announced to the consultant that core teams "could be built here." Upon seeking complete clarification of the statement he had just heard from Jo Ann, the comment was reiterated and confirmed, and her permission sought and obtained for her to declare upfront to the entire group at the next training session what she had said in private. The day of presentation came and Jo Ann was interviewed in the class. She stated her wish and desire that core teams be formed in their departments and that she was going to be an active participant. The effects were nothing short of astounding. By far the majority of her peers and leaders accepted and anticipated the core team formation procedure, and that procedure was earnestly begun.

Several years have passed now, and Jo Ann has been promoted; in fact, currently she serves as a leader within her department. To her list of duties has been added more responsibilities because she is a solution thinker and provider, helping others to achieve as she does. It was from a director that Jo Ann's current status was learned, and this led Jo Ann and me to engage in an interview, to look back, evaluate, and project. Here are the answers to the questions in her interview:

1. Why are strong relationships in the workplace important?

Jo Ann answered that strong working relationships affect the work of every member of the group or team. When each team member values good relationships, the feelings of each team member are taken into consideration. Further, each person's goal matches the unit or team's goal, which is to complete all the tasks with everyone pitching in, always ready to lend a hand when needed. While happiness may be hard to quantify, having a healthy environment promotes happiness, and people look forward to coming to work with acceptance and preparation, ready to go and complete a project. Problem solving is more within reach. Jo Ann stated, "The unit will be able to identify specific barriers to collaboration and common methods to overcome them." Well said! Clearly, cooperation in the fulfillment of cohesive and agreed goals is the uppermost result of strong relationships, and Jo Ann serves on a team that proves this.

2. How well do core teams work when leadership has committed to them?

"Having the knowledge and feeling that your supervisor and manager are willing to support your team makes it easier for the member to say what they feel and at the same time work with an assurance that you have a supervisor and manager who are committed to stay behind you no matter what happens." Support from the leadership is not optional when a core team works as well as it can. Further, "Core team members will have a feeling that you have a safe environment for others to communicate. Loyalty will be built within the group, division and department. When you feel that your leaders are committed with the team, the members are encouraged and motivated to work and share ideas for the betterment of a team." This is living proof, and it thrives.

3.   *What kinds of growth have you experienced?*

Jo Ann stated that after attending the Growing Core Teams (GCT) training offered by Creative Team Resources Group, Inc. (CTRG), "...I was able to apply what I learned by being a good role model with my staff and supervisor." Role model development begins with a decision to become a contributor based on enduring principle, no matter the position or title. Often this decision builds upon values already present. "Basically, even prior to attending the GCT training, I had been dedicated with what I do, even considering myself a workaholic, loyal, a good team member and a good leader. I did not hesitate to teach and train whatever knowledge I had gained related to my job. I think it became a plus and one of my qualities, why people looked up to me." Leadership that is modeled becomes molded into the life of another.

Jo Ann explained that the best thing that has happened to her is that as she has grown, because of her decision to engage, her growth processes became her investments in others! In other words, she included others in her processes of development. Opportunity for promotion followed for her and now those people she leads seek her guidance for problem solving in their group. Respect has been present and more has been earned because she and her team value the relationships that continually are invested within her group, division and department.

This has been a good journey for Jo Ann, her leaders, and followers. As a significant closing statement she said, "I thank you, my supervisors, managers and co-workers for the good experience." No wonder she's a leader of a core team that provisions well!

Chapter 5:
Compliment Your Complement

To develop a mixture that produces a product that is stronger in its collective constitution than if evaluated only on the basis of the quality of its individual parts, the leader who devises the groupings for the core teams knows that each element has to be respected for what it really is, and the value-added it brings to the whole solution. The organizer treasures the diversity his or her group or team represents. The group organizer views each separate element and decides what kind of proper placement each may require to build the strongest opportunities for success. All the elements should not look, sound, or act and produce the same; were they identical, there would be no mixture, of course.

You and your group should treasure uniqueness, give and make room for inclusion of variety. Differences in people, including their personalities, educations, experiences and environments can become strong contributors to a work culture where genuine appreciation and respect are the rules and not the exceptions. These positive attributes and cooperative complements deserve recognition and places to grow, where desires to create wholeness through working together well don't impede; rather, they assist.

There is a perceived threat here, and it goes back to desire.

The threat is that the more divergence present, the more opportunity for disconnect, dysfunction or downright failure is also present—if handled improperly. While partly true, that conclusion rests on whether or not the mixtures are formed according to viable standards, as shown in the last chapter. Where standards are not utilized as the basis for acclamation and activity, then yes, the threat is no longer merely perceived— it's real and looms large—and may literally materialize with accompanying explosions. But where standards comprise an agreed foundation, this threat is diminished, if not eliminated completely, because the group desires to win and will not compromise standards in their efforts. A core team desires well when it agrees on the underpinnings of their beliefs.

Variety of thought, innovation, and creativity—these are sought-after characteristics of a healthy group, and when they are present, their presence and values are closely observed and deeply appreciated. Creative combinations are celebrated as honor to one represents honor to all. Treasure in diversity is not just that diversity is present—it's that it is working and working well, and that all team members are sharing in the journey—its benefits, struggles, achievements, disappointments, failures and wins.

A team that values its diversification and uniqueness is not a static entity consumed with contemplating its own culture, and it is not content with inactive and non-productive sessions, singing yet another refrain of "Kum Ba Yah," or chanting "Ohhmmm" while members sway in concentric circles, holding hands. In fact, this group rarely sits around contemplating anything for a very long time, period. This is an active cluster, dynamic and aggressive, because they are designed that way. This is a working solution tasked with creating success models. While they understand that deep thinking and group camaraderie are important, talking and communicating about plans vital, they also know that action within verified time lines is supreme. Action is the place where authenticity is proven by superior management and excellent provision, coming only from hard work. These people are busy accomplishing important duties because they are supposed to, and they are doing them in right and honorable ways.

This group may be so busy that they rely heavily on a leader or team coordinator to set a pace and provide a continuing focus. Part of complimenting this complement of individuals may be helping them keep the main thing the main thing. Recognize it because it is true: one tendency for creative folks and innovative people working together is that there is so much freedom and innovation, they can veer off a central task and often start wandering down bunny trails. Discipline is required from each contributor in holding his or her person accountable for his or her tasks. Note this in depth, take it to heart: the responsibility is not in holding each other accountable, where one person takes the liability for reminding and evaluating the actions of another. The responsible accountability is owned by each, for his or her individual actions and contributions. Each member monitors himself or herself. This is an important difference. It will make, or severely inhibit, the growth of faithfulness to duty and authenticity of character when applied across the board.

Each person who is part of the workable solutions relies on a clear, present, and consistently updated understanding of the value of his or her contributions and sees where his or her part fits into the whole, demonstrating the inherent value this piece supplies. The goal must always be illuminated, the reasons behind the goal ever presently understood and agreed upon, and the plans to achieve the goals constantly in the forefront of motivation and method.

The role of solid leaders and followers who understand and appreciate the values of each team member—in their persons and contributions, and the central goals they are called to fulfill—is to keep the core team participants focused on the big "whys" of their projects, so that attentions are set and distractions diffused. This is often easier stated than accomplished. Intrusions and considerations come con-stantly—change orders, new laws, fresh people, innovative ideas, altered timelines, imposed corporate demands, stodgy people, old and worn methods, aggregate and aggravating financial considerations, expansion factors, rookie folks too afraid to risk, company growth, decline in the markets, new ownership, unresolved conflicts, wrong assumptions and conclusions, old ownership—you get the point. Business is flooded with wanted and unwanted waves of chance and change. This fact is simply a part of what makes businesses necessarily inclusive of unwanted busy-ness, as well as collections of profitable enterprises.

So, handling the intrusions becomes a need to be dealt with. It is certainly preferable to hoping the intrusions will just go away. They won't. The question is not whether incursions have to be confronted, but how.

There are three "Lights on the Heights" that help core team members concentrate on most-important agendas, encouraging them not to be dissuaded from the essentials. Leaders and group followers use these to illuminate their paths toward building industrial strength solutions. The "Lights on the Heights" are Character, Competence, and Choice. Notice how each can and should be included in building success.

Counting Character

One of the greatest compliments any core team member can give another, regardless of title or position, is affirming right character seen in deeds and depth. It simply goes to the essence of the situation and the person, where the center of the thing, or the soul of the being, is affirmed for its goodness and right standing.

Affirmation of character must be honestly given when the evidences of the contributions and the person are noteworthy. This is a joyful exercise, one in which healthy people often engage. It is not personality-pushed; it is decision-driven. Realizing worth is not a challenge; it's a choice.

Healthy teams possess people who contribute much from right motives, and they are easy to recognize. Candidly, however, the recurring issue is this: solid people and what they perform may be simply overlooked. They and their contributions are just "assumed" by others because their contributions happen repeatedly. Recognition and heart-felt praise are not offered freely and often enough because the team simply gets used to excellence, or in seeing it, fails to see the beauty in the act of affirming it.

Recognition, at its core, is all about seeing evidences, taking effort, and making time to reward right things and right people in right time frames, not from a sense of obligation, but from a desire to build up the "who" and the "do" when the affirmation is most appropriate; not waiting so long after an event that the person being recognized is going, or gone, literally.

When a team member is honestly grateful for the co-workers and what they produce, he or she realizes a high value in the exercise of giving praise, as well as seeing the causes for it. The praise flows freely, uninhibited by stiffness, or stifled by assumed and silent conclusions when it is true. It is truly motivated from the one who wants to affirm. This kind of recognition is born of legitimate need, from giver and receiver. When warmly offered, it is most often gratefully welcomed by the people who are making the working solutions work well.

We conclude that some believe, and therefore practice, this idea: true gratitude, as an attitude and action, may be easier to possess than express. But let's look deeper into this mistaken and misshapen idea. Team participants who value the significance of gratitude understand that it is required of healthy groups who are engaged in solution provision. Why? Because character counts, a lot—and when in evidence, it should be overtly affirmed. The discipline to give affirmation, because it is a right and proper gift, outshines the lame excuses for holding it back.

True thankfulness seeks its own ways of acknowledging that for which it is thankful. Groundless excuses for inaction, like, "I just didn't get around to it" or "I really need to tell him I appreciate his efforts" are replaced with proactive thinking and genuine praise that counts and can be counted upon. Any momentary discomfort in taking the time to write an email, send a card, pick up the phone or stop by a work station is substituted with a focus not on what it takes but on what it gives to the other person who contributes that for which praise is offered.

Counting character realigns attention away from the person who needs to give it, to the person who is due its approbation, who has earned, through his or her labors, that for which genuine appreciation should be shown. This disciplined giving is required of anyone who wants to share the winnings of all those on the core team who are working together. It is not drudgery. It is a delight.

Rewarding Competence

Doing a good job is not its own reward, as though just the accomplishment were, in total, the end of the discussion. Doing admirable work is a positive attribute for anyone who is working hard, and certainly has some built-in incentives and motivations as part of getting a job accomplished well. But it doesn't stop there, nor should it.

Building successful solutions includes presenting tangible rewards for achievement, because the act of rewarding demonstrates respect. Payment honors the competence of the achiever, recognizes the applied knowledge required to do a job, and compensates the provider for admirable contribution.

Commensurate pay is one of many ways to say thanks and pass along earned and deserved worth. The industrial strength solutions mandate is to always pay more than what is expected to all who provide more than what they are paid to give. Further, the mandate requires that one does not complete a job merely to the agreed level of excellence; rather, the level of excellence expected is actually exceeded whether or not the extra contributions are overtly noticed. Rewarding competence is seen when payer and payee both "do just a little more" than the standard, to let the other person know they are more important than what they do. It is an exchange always welcomed, and should be characteristic of a core team lifestyle.

It "costs" so little to produce and give more—in both lucre and labor. But it says much more when the joy of achievement and affirmation is passed from one to another. Try this the next time you wish to say thanks, and you are the one writing the check, or paying the bill for the services rendered: give a bonus, a little extra, in the form of cash or a gift certificate, and make sure that in the budget you manage, there is room for doing this.

"If you do it for one do you have to do it for all?" Where did the notion of entitlement and forced levels of compensation come from? Classifications are important in the work place, of course, and levels of pay for levels of work are right and should be clearly defined and articulated, but they should not be the final determiners, setting immovable limits that deny opportunity for giving and paying more, if so desired, from people who understand the value of rewarding competence. Recognitions of the heart and the hand transcend such artificial limits as these, and should.

If you are a worker who wants to strengthen your contributions beyond measure, then make sure you don't just adequately fulfill a requirement of a task—exceed it. If your work is behind the scenes, then make sure that you are not the one who informs the rest of the team that it was you who contributed more. Your benefits will follow in more ways than you can count, hence the use of the phrase "beyond measure," if you don't trumpet your own tip. Money is only one measure of success. Many more endurable measures are worth your silence when your contributions are not in full view, but still contribute greatly.

If you are the employee, give the extra effort required to assure more excellence than is expected in what you do. In doing so you reward the competence of the leader who placed you in a position to excel, and your competence will be compensated as the products you manufacture go above merely meeting expectations to giving the consumer more than he or she ever paid for.

In building solutions for success there is no substitute for rewarding competence—both as a payer and payee, an employer and employee. Everyone shares the benefits whether sources of labor and lucre are known, or not. Plus, the end-user receives more and likely ends up purchasing additional quantities of what is sold, or brings new customers into the fold, because rewarding competence builds confidence, all the way around, all the time. Contributory core team members reward competence, and are rewarded for it themselves.

Celebrating Choices

There are many little choices that carry with them diminished consequence when measured against more weighty subjects. What I choose for breakfast this morning is probably not as important as the institution of higher education I decide to attend. But this illustration points up a fairly universal temptation every worker or team member faces: concentrating on minors while majors are waiting to be solved.

In great organizations dedicated effort is expended to keep the main thing central. It doesn't mean the participants aren't open to new ideas; rather, it means that the new ideas have something to do with the reason the organization exists in the first place. Healthy expansion is possible when success has been demonstrated repeatedly in the areas for which a group is working primarily, for which they were formed. Ideas that go beyond this framework usually require a new frame. While new frames are welcomed, they are developed better if they come about as a result of faithful contributions preceding them.

Choices make the difference between success and failure, and this is understood. What most folks don't ponder enough is how important their daily choices are, even including relatively small ones that may make or break quality and quantity of their work. Regardless of size, every choice matters. The smaller ones should make jobs go easier, the larger ones set major parameters of success and achievement. All, however, are dedicated to a single focus: to build industrial strength solutions. Working workable solutions, that is, provisioning the people who provide their services to accomplish agreed goals, carries with it the encouragement and dedication to keep the choices right, within their proper frameworks, for the right reasons, regardless of their size.

Cumulative good choices, small or great, yield strong results over time. When their results come, the celebrations should come, too. A sharp leader or member sees results, seizes them, and brings them to the attention of the group of providers, pointing up specifics of why the choices were good, what the great results are, and how the purchaser or end-user has been fulfilled. Observers are aware, and their awareness provides open doors to celebrations.

Remember that "workable solutions" are the combinations of people that make products or services come to fruition. They are the people dedicated to seeing and following the lights on the heights—the three factors and motivators that above all the activity, keep the people attuned to attaining their goals.

"Lights on the Heights" is a phrase that requires us to get a visual. It is this: a lighthouse on a rocky shore, a beacon on a hill issuing signals that penetrate the darkness for all to see. Character, competence and choice are these lights. The team's existence and levels of productivity require that they are recognized, affirmed, and honored. Putting them above the daily activity gives them the prominence they require to serve their people well. Counting character, rewarding competence and celebrating choices are actions desired and designed to stimulate, motivate, keep a group centered on target, and congratulate the successes that are sure to come.

Complimenting your complement simply means that in your group or unit you and others affirm the folks who do their jobs, whether you are the leader or a follower. You and others on your team will do this as the team treasures the variety each person brings to its organization, notices and rewards character, honors competence and good choices, and uses these attributes of contribution as inspirations to firmly stay the course the group has agreed composes their destinations and destiny.

Industrial strength solutions come from the inside out before they ever are offered or imposed from the outside in. Build internally first. A staff should be the recipients of the good of the organization long before the customers receive their portions. In fact, the customer will be served better if that service originates from a well-served staff.

How often the reverse is practiced, and companies struggle. In a typical organization, people are frequently used, then used up, disposed of or discarded. Such is not the case in an organization where winners who are part of a solution (mixture) with other winners possess and demonstrate a sole and soul-inspired goal of providing strong workable solutions based on deep and earnest desires to belong to something greater than their own selves.

"Lights on the Heights"
Factors and Motivators to Help People Attain Their Goals

Counting Character	Rewarding Competence	Celebrating Choices
Affirm goodness and right standing.	Build confidence by giving and paying more.	When results become known, have a party.

The Learning Experience

Doug is the General Manager of a thriving business, employs 35 people, and the enterprise is clearly a success in less than ten years of its existence. When the business was formed, one or two people at the top set policy and imposed their leadership on the rest of the staff. To assure compliance, tasks were often set ahead of people's importance in their thinking and operations.

When the business started to mature, the owners made a decision to integrate the lessons surrounding core teams along with the expansion of the enterprise. Applications of values-driven principles caused all participants involved in the Core Team training and one-on-one consultation sessions to re-evaluate their individual as well as group levels of participation and raise their own standards. There was general recognition that this process was likely going to take some quality and quantity time to implement, and leadership determined that the price to pay would be worth the end result. Education and application of principles were infused into the day-to-day activities for a time frame spanning over two years. Upon review, some clear lessons can be extrapolated from the experience.

According to Doug, "As we have grown, our people have become more important than their jobs. Now our people are integral parts of the decision and policy-making processes. As in any group, some have progressed better than others." This is true, and is an evaluation worth remembering as you and your core teams count character, reward competence and celebrate good choices.

Doug, as the central guidance giver, has tried to model his leadership after the Great Communicator, Ronald Reagan, who, while he was the one who could deliver the punch, would obtain input from his people and then make his decision and declare his policy. The key is involving the people to create ownership. Now, in Doug's organization, core issues and their implementation include input coming from greater commitment, and buy-in from multiple people on multiple teams. Broader-based ownership is the result.

Doug has stated that his most significant struggle, as his

people have grown, is when to lead from the old paradigm of "doing it himself," if ever. Patience is stretched and perseverance needed when he gives the freedom to act and sees setbacks because an employee doesn't make it to agreed expectations. The clear and ever-present danger "to take over" appears when Doug yearns to fix the problems himself. How often should he "rescue" his people? Should he rescue them at all? Should he take back duties that they are not grasping yet, in terms of leadership and follow-through? The challenge, simply stated, is this: understanding what to take back, if anything, or what to leave alone and let the team learn by going through the difficulty. The consideration to guide instead of fix problems forms the basis for mature and better decisions that the team and Doug exercise when they choose to embrace challenges as a team, as opposed to the leader taking them back.

In our interview, Doug articulated a list of results that he had witnessed first-hand over the course of our engagement together. This list is significant because it represents a no-holds-barred view of reality of team instruction and application. Doug stated, "When a team is turned upon a new philosophy, at least one new to that team, we can expect some of these results:

1. Resistance
2. Excuses
3. Buy-in
4. Mixed signals
5. Desire but not ability
6. Hidden ability that comes to the forefront
7. Struggles for authority and position as an overbearing leader has to relinquish control in light of people who are growing
8. Satisfaction when a person of capability and desire combines both attributes with a growing understanding of essential core values agreement, and becomes a better, if not a "new" leader

9. Self-esteem and trust-building within the people "beneath," which can be threatening to a structure that doesn't promote growth
10. Recognition that the ability to "replace" one's self takes a strong will and an even stronger character that sees the benefits beyond the struggle
11. Learning the lesson that changing behavior takes time and perseverance
12. Realizing that negativity becomes more evident in our weaker players, but can be replaced by positive action in more maturing individuals who encourage them."

Whenever a team and its leadership make the firm commitment to grow in its values and their applications in daily operations they are challenged to develop and achieve new goals because maturity demands it. Doug articulated three primary goals of the core teams in his organization, developed as a result of the company's desire to help people attain their aspirations for themselves and improve their job performance:

Continue to strengthen and expand teams and their respective capabilities, while…

Ascertaining individuals' desires and abilities to continue to grow, on the basis of…

What they say and what they do in a pattern that reinforces whether an employee wants solutions and takes the initiative to provide for them, or conversely, chooses to live in the status quo, remaining in the problems that they are unwilling to solve.

I asked Doug as we wrapped up the conversation: "Do they get it?" His answer: "Problems are reduced when excuses are replaced with potential and follow-through." They are clearly learning to become greater contributors as Doug is growing to become an even stronger leader.

Achieving unified strength in any group is not automatic. Setting parameters and reaching desired levels of endurance and resiliency take dedicated efforts and a continued focus on character, competence and choice. Strength in these energetic endeavors is a condition, but is not conditional in the sense that it is moved or motivated by circumstances. It is a decision, one based on desire, as are so many of the elements in the mixture of success.

Study the chart below to see how energetic endeavors can be compared to movement that occurs only upon a leader's constant and direct involvement. A core team who wants to contribute as part of an industrial strength solution will choose initiative because they are centered on what is primary, keeping the main thing the main thing.

Indecision vs. Initiative Chart

Initiative is the mark of a team that doesn't just wait for solutions; rather, it yearns for the opportunity to engage in a process of solution provision where members create, present and, upon approval, implement solutions that work. Look at the differences. In the first illustration, indecision promotes waiting for someone (usually an overworked and micromanaging leader) to give constant direction, to which involvement is applied and a task is completed. The job gets done, but these workers are task-providers only.

Indecision: no direction... ⟶ Involvement: completing tasks.

Initiative: creating solutions... ⟶ Implementation: ownership of a job well done.

In the second example the core team takes the initiative in recognizing a problem and owns the creation of its solution. When approved, the team unifies to implement their solutions. Again, the job gets done, but this process is stronger because *it includes the people that own the problem in the design and implementation of the problem's solution.* They are engaged in an agreed, focused and verifiable commitment, and cooperate fully in its achievement.

Chapter 6:
Strength Is a Condition—
But It Is Not Conditional

Recall that the key element to building industrial strength solutions is desire. Desires are born of dreams. Dreams originate from innovative minds that yearn to make a difference. Together, innovative minds, dreams and desires initiate choices that give rise to actions that achieve strength and contribute to resilience. Strength as a condition of existence is the product of this important process of development and is not easily affected and rarely moved at all by circumstances or chance occurrences. Indeed, strength borne on this process changes the effects of the circumstances it touches.

If you want your group to be strong, how willing are you and your people to perform the necessary functions and exercises to witness strength result? What will be the indicators that the desired strength condition has been achieved?

The Unhealthy Mixture

Strife at the top infused the office. The tension was hard to avoid. Twenty employees composed the staff of this small service company. Their cramped work cubicles were located in a tiny building spread over three floors. It all felt squished and squashed. What happened on one floor was not unknown to those on the other floors, in short order. They were tight in location, and often tight on funds. Most importantly, they were lacking in quality relationships. The combination of these factors may have been largely due to the rapid growth they experienced at the outset of creating their company called "Showcase," which had begun as a firm dedicated to the delivery of excellence, or so it was initially said, and believed.

Character traits loom large in small spaces, and in times of stress in this organization, true characters were revealed. When disagreements arose at the top between the CEO, COO and CFO, and they often did, these disagreements became apparent through means of expression that included small attempts at tearing down each other publicly, talking behind each other's backs, and then morphed quickly into overt displays of disrespect, argumentation that departed from the issues at hand and devolved upon personalities, or just plain expressions of dislike with corresponding and blatant disregard of how any of this discomfiture might be affecting other staff. No matter which floor on which the arguments and conflicts occurred, this show was creating an unpleasant place to work as bottom-dwelling attitudes and actions permeated its once invigorated environment.

A series of interactions, rising in intensity, served as beacon signals to the rest of the staff that the parties were at odds, and that their internal strife was growing, maybe beyond repair. Interestingly, these signals were seen in their styles of humor— thick with sarcasm, mockery and destructive put-downs. Objects of ridiculing humor employed on a mounting basis were other people, a person's mistakes, or a group's embarrassment. Taken initially as superficial nudging or "making fun," the biting and bashing multiplied until no one was being fooled any longer as to the real purpose of their onslaught: destruction of one by another.

Over time, plans and processes started to become severely

impacted by the mounting dysfunction; instead of "looking the other way," the employees began to take sides, and the effects of this negative networking increased daily. In instance after instance the pressure mounted. It wasn't a matter of just being noticeable any longer—it had become an endurance contest.

Finally, after about six months of fairly continuous momentum, it all came to an ugly climax. The explosion occurred like this: the COO had initiated a plan for expansion of the customer base, involving a certain funding expenditure, and the CEO's agreement had been obtained for the procedure to begin. Action steps and time lines were established, and movement forward had commenced within the rest of staff. At a critical point of implementation where contacts with customers would be affected, the CFO halted all movement; he had found some point relative to budgeting and financial reporting that he didn't like. None of the staff were given any reasons why—they all were simply commanded by the CFO, in no uncertain terms, to cease and desist from all activity of implementation of the new customer acquisition plan until the problem, as he saw it, could be remedied.

Upon learning of the setback, the COO exploded. He literally marched like a Nazi through the corridors, spreading his venom on all the floors, up and down and around the offices, cornering anyone who would listen, censuring the CFO (using derision and contempt in his choice of names of this gentleman), proclaiming that "HE" had blocked the plan—he had blocked the plan—he had blocked the plan! The walls and halls were permeated with his screaming and childish antics. This demonstration, with its absence of self-control, was disgusting to everyone unfortunate enough to witness it, an embarrassment to a new height of social and personal (not to mention personnel) dysfunction, that left soured stomachs and "get me outta here!" attitudes and comments in its wake. What little respect the COO may have had among some staff to this point quickly evaporated into the contemptuous atmosphere he had fostered with his displays of gross and grotesque immaturity.

Seen as an isolated incident this possibly could have passed into the heap of singular and unfortunate relational interactions with which the company had become all too familiar in its short term of life. However, for Showcase, this one was the proverbial straw on the camel's back that finally exceeded the weight it could bear.

It was true that the CFO's power play had not only stopped the plan of customer base expansion, but it also had robbed the plan-making process of some desperately needed credibility. However, the foolishness of the reaction of the COO simply demonstrated, in a blatant format, how immature these leadership people really were, and how far their dysfunction had fallen. Indeed, what small degrees of confidence and motivation remained before the outburst simply "left the building" at the conclusion. Loss of respect, frustration, and a sense of "What does it matter anyway?" made staff roll their eyes, shrug their shoulders, and walk away, some leaving for the day in utter repugnance. Several resignations soon followed as those who had decided to depart permanently simply said, "Forget this!" The CEO was humiliated, and tried to "make peace" in a disjointed fashion out of the jagged pieces of the remainder of his employees, but it didn't work. He lost respect in the transaction, too, simply because he had permitted the relational angst to progress to the degree that it had. Everyone had concluded, "It was only a matter of time."

Negative functions tend to showcase negative relationships, and here was fresh evidence of this permutation of truth. No matter if competence was questioned, the more important observation was that soured character had won the day, and the focus of all was affected by these character-deficient, destitute and unfortunate choices.

Not a pretty picture, but unfortunately this is one that companies of varying sizes face too often. The end result, in this case, was that this company and its leadership eventually did not survive. The solutions they could have offered to their customer base, of course, were never known. Their fall was great as was the destruction to the people who formerly worked there. Months, and even years following its demise, people still wondered: "Whatever happened to Showcase?"

You would be correct if you judged that the story of Showcase was a tale of weakness. What cannot be known in this telling, however, is the strength that each of the primary players brought to the mix of people when the company was originally formed and they were initially retained. Were they to have acted on their strengths and chosen a purposeful application of The Four Decisions and The Four Standards, the results likely would have been very different, and the company still in business.

Strength is a condition, a state of being—but it is not conditional. Just because strong people are present does not guarantee that their combined strengths will be mixed in such a way as to produce longevity and good working environments. In their collective operations they may not automatically produce strong results; they may indeed cause destruction.

If strength were conditional then that idea would indicate that all would be well as long as favorable circumstances were present. Its opposite must therefore also be true, that if strength were conditional, when circumstances were negative, cooperation would cease to exist. It is true that while many organizations operate mostly on reaction to good and bad circumstances, this clearly does not indicate strength when their stories are told; this demonstrates weakness, showcasing a team or group that is tossed by waves and whims of whatever comes along.

Strength is not conditional, is not based on positive and negative circumstances for its effectiveness or longevity. Strength is a condition that firmly withstands, regardless. If strength is wanted, then all parties purposefully choose higher motivations of working well, no matter the conditions, personalities and work styles involved. Strength comes from firm and deliberate choices based on mutual and agreed desires.

Strength as a condition is chosen within an understanding that each member might have to compromise a little on the minors while they continue to agree wholeheartedly on the majors. They uphold their standards and values and lock arms to win their goals. They refuse to let surface concerns throw them off primary tasks. They put character, competence and choice up front, knowing that these inspire. They are free and encouraged to compliment their complements, and do so willingly, and often.

The decision to position strength in this way comes almost exclusively from what people declare they want. What people want is an illustration of what they value. Even where disagreements devolve, if primary core values and accompanying systems of operation show core essence agreement, then when minor adjustments have to be made they will be made free of questioning character or demonstrations of core value discontinuance.

The process is more important than the product; the people are more important than the production. Core teams that espouse these truths are far less prone to demon-administrations as in the Showcase story above—indeed, the results of their genuine co-operation generate positive impacts on those who see and are touched, and strength as a choice of condition, and not a conditional happenstance, will be the state in which contributions toward success are made.

Desires for strength become foundations for choices that bring stability and resilience over time. The phrase "over time" is important: mixing these solutions may not bring about instantaneous results, but the results are sure to come when the process of combination includes agreement on the essences.

If strength in solution provision begins with a choice, then what are the elements that should be considered in creating the most durable workable solutions? Three are identified here: Positional Perspectives, Personnel Placements, and Performance Procedures. It takes hard and diligent work to establish and use these, but in the context of creating industrial strength solutions, their contributions outweigh the costs of the work to engage them. Remember, it begins with desire. If strength is what we want, then here are some solid ideas on how to choose to get it. Consider these elements of mixing well in building your industrial strength solutions.

Positional Perspectives

See what you want before you start. If this goal is not apparent from the outset, take the time and work with the people who will establish it definitively. You may wish to form a Goal Designation Task Force (GDTF) to come up with clearly stated descriptions regarding the constitution of strong solutions to problems or issues, setting a framework in place to which others can contribute ideas. The GDTF not only outlines what the expected results will be, but also charts the benefits, those who will receive them, and in what desired time frame.

Writing desired perspectives down and then distributing them for broader agreement and buy-in is an essential activity for the GDTF. Commitment to planning carefully will help begin the process of developing strength.

Here's a sample outline of the GDTF agenda:
1. The goal of our solution provision: the results we expect
2. The benefits of achieving our goal
3. The desired time frame for initiation and completion
4. The action steps we will engage
5. The standards of effectiveness to which we will adhere
6. The people who will participate
7. The correction measures we will employ
8. The celebrations we will enjoy

The GDTF designs and presents plans to the broader group for ratification and institution. It is an exciting prospect when the plans are approved and the initiation dates set. The perspectives and outlined assignments created by the GDTF contribute needed definition, first-step motivation and eager anticipation toward movement to the next action: Personnel Placements.

Personnel Placements

Placing people is best accomplished through a process that recognizes where they most desire involvement. This process establishes not only who will do the job, but provides closure on what needs to be done. There is a temptation to merely identify tasks and find people to fill them without due regard for the interest, capability and passion of the people who are to be involved. Go the other way. Identify the people's contribution areas first; then place them in the appropriate roles that will fulfill the jobs, and the people, while the jobs are underway.

This is global positioning and specific strength pinpointing. These are accomplished simultaneously and cooperatively within broader *need* (task) and detailed *deed* (personnel or relationship) areas. A large and encompassing need will be accompanied by certain unique requirements of task fulfillment. Under a broader understanding of what has to be done, the deed will fulfill the need in superior fashion with exceptional results — when right people are tasked with doing right jobs because those jobs align well with the passion, interest, education and experience of the person who will do the job.

Part of a leader or influencer's responsibility is to work toward establishing a strong alignment of these two ingredients:

1. Deed <u>and</u> Need (understanding strengths of the people and comprehending the requirements of fulfilling the task)

2. Deed <u>with</u> Need (positioning the best people who will complete the jobs with excellence)

When the need is fully understood, it is then that the focus becomes not just fulfillment in deeds with people who may appear to qualify based solely on competence; rather, on those who authentically demonstrate in their actions, seen from their experience, education, environment, and most of all desire and passion, that they are a good, proper and best fit. Upon this foundation of understanding a workable success solution is developed and, because of the strength of its central and core essence make-up, the combination has the best opportunity to produce best results.

Far too often "Need is King"—and people are acquired and used to fulfill necessary jobs without sufficient attention paid to ascertaining if they are the ones who are best suited to accomplish the Deed. When Need is King alone, the mix of people can become explosive, as it was in Showcase, and destructive over time. In best combinations, Deed and Need should be seen as "peers" because they truly are, and should be positioned cooperatively, in balance.

Taking the time, up front, to find out who the people are, what passions, talents, gifts, experience, education, and environments they bring to the table, can produce not only superior workable solutions built on strength, but happier people in the processes because better people produce better products and problem solutions! When these elements are properly combined and thoughtfully aligned they generate more than what is expected with superior quality thrown in for good measure.

Seek to connect your people well within relationships and work responsibilities. The more connectivity between deed and need, the stronger is the mix and the potential for the greater contribution as these people cooperate from balanced perspectives. Put deed completion first, and when it is properly positioned, need fulfillment with excellence is more likely to follow.

This process takes time and energy. It is not a quick fix, nor is it an instant pudding mix. Putting these truths into an operational paradigm too rapidly can be likened to trying to enjoy the cake before it has even been baked. Wise counsel says to take it one step at a time, and move as your organization allows you to move; but by all means, move.

Whenever a new project is presented and a workable solution group or core team is formed to complete a job, you are encouraged to take right steps. Perhaps consider using the sample outline below as a guide. Strive to put principle into practice and become a model of effective planning and purposed procedure. Obtain necessary agreements and allow sufficient time for development, utilizing these tools.

Create two lists, as illustrated below:
1. Member Name and Interest/Passion (Deed Areas)
2. Tasks to Accomplish (Need Areas)

Then use the Placement Grid to match a group member's interest, passion, experience and fulfillment areas to the required tasks. As part of the process of matching, define jobs specifically, create detailed assignments, provide needed instruction and tools for success, and determine time lines for fulfillment.

List 1: Deed Areas
Member, Interest/Passion, and Experience/Fulfillment

Member Name	Interest/Passion Areas	Experience/Fulfillment
1. Member Name		
2. Member Name		
3. Member Name		

List 2: Need Areas
Tasks to Accomplish

Category	Job Description	Assignment	Tools to Succeed	Time Line
1. Task Overview--				
2. Task Overview--				
3. Task Overview--				

The completion of Lists 1 and 2 allow the leader or manager to insert the findings into the Placement Grid. The exercise of working through the development of List 1 and List 2, and the use of the Placement Grid should be shared by all group members who will be affected in order to create proper ownership of duty and responsibility, including sharing authority and accountability. Involving the entire team lets the participants know they are vital parts of the process. Due diligence and respect is offered for their Deed strengths, and Need areas assignments more accurately reflect what these people have declared are the areas in which they can and will perform well, giving each other and their customers (the party for whom the project is being done) the excellence born of ownership and dignity. In a workable solution like this, industrial strength is not only possible—it is an expected outcome, and the product deliverables are superior.

The Placement Grid is a tool to chart the line-up of people and their respective functional tasks. This chart should be adapted to the specific needs of the work group and the individuals in it. Obviously the sample below is just that—a sample. You or your core team leader will want to customize a Placement Grid to fit your organizational and project-specific language, overall goals, and particulars.

Placement Grid

Name/ID	Interests/Passions	Tasks	Assignments/Tools	Time Line
1. Member Name				
2. Member Name				
3. Member Name				

Placement Grid Key:
Name/ID: Identification of the person who is to be assigned actions.
Interests/Passions: specific areas on which a member wants to work within categorized Need Areas that most accurately align with Deed fulfillment.
Tasks: those jobs that fall within a category that is close to, or matches a member's interests or passions.
Assignment/Tools: specific job duties given to the member with sufficient instructions and necessary tools.
Time Line: the date and duration of the assignment, including due date.

Performance Procedures

"What is my job description?" "I have worked here for 'x' months (or years) and still don't have a job description." "I want to finish those job descriptions for my staff before their next (or first) review." "So-and-so was just hired, and starts Monday; this old job description needs to be reconstructed. Would you do it?" "A job description for this position hasn't even been developed, and we really need one." "No job description was created because there have been too many changes." "I've never even heard of one for what I do."

Who should design a job description, and when should it be designed? The usual answer is that the employer or supervisor, who has the job or position to fill, should be responsible for the document's creation. Further, this line of thinking states that the job description should be in place before a new hire is sought. In most cases, the employer looks for the best or most qualified person based on competence and imposes a pre-designed job description onto that person, often as part of the interview process, or in its aftermath. Sometimes job descriptions are late in development or never exist, but business goes on. With an unclear or absent job description, an undercurrent of unrealized clarity and lack of understanding can breed and sow discontent over time. Too many people have faced and lived in this situation for far too long.

Let's take an alternative view. Building industrial strength solutions requires a different and better focus, one inclusive not of just the job to be done and finding the person to fill it, but also of starting with the right person who is discovered to be the best candidate, who, because of combined relational and functional qualifications, is most equipped to fulfill the jobs that need to be done. This is not a word game; this is intentional alignment of best people first for best deliverables next, yielding fulfilled core team members who are placed correctly *because they are part of the placement process*. Here the job description is not pre-imposed on the person; the person is included in its design and implementation. Instead of handing a new hire or potential hire a job description into which the person has to fit, the new or potential hire helps design up to 50% of its composition to assure that it will fit, based on the quality of the person first, and the expectation of job completion next.

Look for the right people—then assure that the job can be done. Engage in a cooperative effort to generate job descriptions that not only accomplish need, but also include right people who will perform the deed. This is a balanced perspective. And if balance here is desired, then equal weight will be placed on the job and the person who is the candidate for it.

This focus represents tremendous attitude and aptitude viewpoint changes. The new hire, or new-to-a-position employee, or the employee who has been working for any length of time in the absence of a clear job description, gets to understand fully what constitutes a win in the position considered because he or she is involved in creating the win's definition and its associated parameters of success. The job requirement in terms of task completion is considered from a holistic relational and functional point of view because the right people, who are closest to the job, are helping do the considering.

Some leaders or managers may see this idea as radical or an illustration of the softer underbelly side of business "feeling." Nothing could be further from the truth. Correctly positioning people on the basis of passion and potential, character and competence, builds the kind of strengths great core teams desire. The process is not easy, takes more up-front time, it may be more costly initially, but in the long run produces greater end results. In this paradigm of winning, ownership of the job is not assumed or hoped for; rather, it is diligently factored in, and that ownership creates fertile grounds of success. In this process imposition is substituted with inclusion, a stronger form and formula. Indeed, success is more assured and confidently acted upon because people, whose desires, passions, and competencies are matched, are employed more fully to complete the necessary deeds to take tasks to finalization.

> Look for the right people—then assure that the job can be done. Engage in a cooperative effort to generate job descriptions that not only accomplish need, but also include right people who will perform the deed.

The real problem here, if there is one, is that this new focus, and hence some new ways of job description design, agreement, assignment and implementation can, and likely will, take a longer time, consume more energy, and will cost more than most employers or managers may really want to pay. It's simply easier to hire and position people "the other way."

Thoughts and phrases like, "There is work to be done, so let's get it done." "Do you want a job?" "Do you want to do this job?" "Can you do this job?" are replaced with considerations like this: "We have a great candidate and we have a job position to fill. Let's see if his or her strengths match the job. If the strengths match the requirements, it's a win. If they don't, and we still believe we have the right person, let's give this person another position. We will keep looking for the right person to fill the other role." Some would argue that this elongated procedure is a waste of time. Consider this: creating good solutions that last should take time and, if a leader or core team captain wants to structure strong workable solutions, this time of investigation and implementation is required, if not mandated, and will pay good dividends. Is your team willing to consider this way of thinking and acting?

Tools can be used to help fashion a job description, prepare an employee for a review, and help the processes to be as productive as possible. One tool is a form called the Personnel Review and Planning Document (PRPD), and another is the Position Account and Contribution Evaluation (PACE) form. As forms go, the layout and content of both should not be complicated, but their designs should be tailored to fit the needs of your group. When they are used as an outline of description and evaluation of relational strengths and functional accomplishment, they can be powerful and effective instruments.

A sample of the first form, the PRPD, is shown in its entirety on pages 217 and 218. Its instructions indicate that it is to be used in advance of a review, for which the second form, PACE, can be utilized. You are welcome to use the PRPD, adapting it to your own needs. Permission is granted for photocopying the document, altering it to your specifications, and using it within your environment and applications. If photocopied, please state the following: "Used with permission of Creative Team Resources Group, Inc. (CTRG), www.ctrg.com."

The Position Account and Contribution Evaluation (PACE) form

The second form, the Position Account and Contribution Evaluation (PACE) is described here. Of course, you can choose your own name for it if an alternate is more suitable. You are encouraged to take the description and custom-design it for your use. However it is constituted, its design should include two primary factors of contribution to the workplace that are equal in importance and equable in application. The first is relationship, which, as has been said, is defined as the decision one makes about, or in support of, another's success. The second is function, defined as the observable actions that corroborate the truth of this decision. Primary to the workings of these definitions is the order in which they must appear on the work scene: relationships (decisions) always precede functions (tasks). Always. A function is the direct evidence of the quality of a relationship. In fact, there is no dysfunction between people that cannot be traced back to a problem in relationship. None. Further, great function between people is a direct product of superior relationships. Placing relationships first will forever improve the understanding of sources and solutions for functional imbalance, or celebrations coming from functional excellence.

Agreement on the networking and symbiotic ties of

relationships and function declares that the same weight should be given to the strength of one as well as the execution of the other. PACE can help achieve an understanding of the balance between the two, both in their representations and applications.

PACE should contain a description of a position, and to evaluate the job quality with which it is associated, should be created to relate and weigh its relationship and function facets uniformly, recognizing they cannot be separated anyway. The form can and should be used in an initial interview, a scheduled evaluation, at an annual and regularly recurring review, and within general assessments whenever needed.

As to its design, there are many templates that can be constructed. As to its content, building industrial strength solutions requires that this document, in whatever configuration it is laid out, provides certain specific grids of measurement at a minimum.

A full description of a template is offered on the following pages, and a sample PACE form is shown beginning on page 219. You are welcome to use the PACE, adapting it to your own needs. Permission is granted for photocopying the document, altering it to your specifications, and using it within your environment and applications. If photocopied, please state the following: "Used with permission of Creative Team Resources Group, Inc. (CTRG), www.ctrg.com." You are encouraged to take the details and design the form that best serves your requirements. Here is a broad overview:

The content of the first half of the PACE form should include a section designed for noting basic identification information and a delineation of a position's summary, focusing on relationships (decisions). The second half should focus on functions (tasks) that the position requires. Its conclusion, related to a pre-determined method of scoring, joins these two categories to present the most complete picture of the balance and interconnectivity of decisions and task fulfillment.

Begin by creating a first section that includes the following important identification information:

1. Company name, logo, and full contact information
2. Title of document: "Position Account and Contribution Evaluation" (PACE)
3. Employee identification information: name, title, number, department or unit (group) of operation, supervisor's name and title
4. Evaluation time frame: initial, 90-day, semi-annual, annual, other
5. Scoring method and PACE score: The scoring system must include a design that places even weight on relationship and function. Your design or selection of methods can be selected from a varied field. An explanation of the scoring system you choose should appear here. For example, if a 100% scoring system is used, a 50% score in relationships and a 50% score in functions would equate to an evaluation that clearly shows balance. If an A, B, C, D, F grading system is employed, then a grade of A would show a superbly healthy combination of both relationship and function, and an F would show a lack of balance in one or the other, or both, demonstrating relational isolation and lack of basic functional contributions, likely resulting in probation or termination.
6. Date of the use of this form
7. Signature lines for use by the employee, supervisor, and other manager(s) if needed, or these can appear at the end of the form as shown in the sample.

The second section describes the position the employee fills. In the wording, include only the essential actions of the position and related performance standards. Essential actions and minimum standards should reflect the organization's Values, Vision, Mission and Message*, its commitment to quality customer care, and its operational efficiencies in expectations of deliverables. Here are examples:

1. Position Summary and Purpose:
   - This section is used to describe the scope of the position the employee holds or for which the candidate is to be hired.
   - It emphasizes agreement and adherence to established company policies and practices, ensures compliance with the organization or division's Employee Handbook in which are included the established company core values.
   - It describes the practice of a work style that reflects the Values, Vision, Mission, and Message of the organization within a thorough understanding of positional authority and accountability.

2. Position Qualifications and Requirements:
   - The minimum qualifications/requirements necessary to adequately perform this position are listed.
   - These could include experience and specialized skills, any necessary educational levels and degrees of experience required to fulfill expectations, and noted achievements relative to qualifications.
   - If the employee needs specific tools (materiel) to accomplish tasks for which he or she is being hired, these are described, also.
   - Requirements and evaluations should include managerial as well as technical abilities if the position necessitates delineation of these factors.
   - Leadership capability, ability, and desire to exceed customer service needs are stated.
   - Additional education: training courses, certifications, letters of completion may be listed as part of the evaluation, encouragement or requirements of growth.

3. Effectiveness Determiners:
   Many factors help the employer and employee weigh and evaluate effectiveness of fulfilling positional responsibilities.

Several are noted as examples:

- Education and training, certifications and registrations
- Descriptions of the impact of the decisions an employee will make on the job: check with your HR professional for exact wording to be employed according to the rules and requirements of your locale, but a statement like this may be helpful: "Unsafe or improper handling and/or delivery of goods and services could jeopardize the company, and this employee, resulting in accompanying loss. Incorrect assessments or errors in judgment may place this employee, or the company, at risk in consideration of ethical, financial, legal or safety considerations." Stress the necessity and worth of good choices and the consequential impacts of decisions.
- How well the employee receives instruction and supervision: what are the attitudes the employee demonstrates when thus engaged, and the degrees of receptivity or rejection shown?
- Networking and interaction of employees with internal and external connections: these constitute additional effectiveness proofs. Internal connections, of course, are the activities this employee has with other employees of the company, regardless of position. External contacts are those with outside providers (vendors) or people who are provisioned by the employee (customers). A statement should be inserted to describe the widest scope of internal and external connectivity to let the employee know the value of his or her impact, influence and investment opportunities within networks with which the employee is involved.
- Physical activities inherent within the functioning of the job: these should be delineated and descriptive assurances given in writing as to the degree of capability the employee possesses to meet what is required. The employee must have knowledge and full understanding of, and agreement with, application of physical

requirements relative to job needs, and the physical stamina to accomplish necessary actions to complete the work described in the role's qualifications and requirements.

- Utilization of time, a vital and additional element: its appropriate use is directly connected to personal and company growth. Efficient and productivity-oriented time management is not optional. Management and utilization of time is weighed carefully as part of the core essence of contribution and a strong consideration factor of effectiveness.

- Safety: it is an important aspect of any workplace environment. Job safety rules that apply to the employee's workspace, and those spaces of others' the employee enters, are noted. Most of these are, or should be, described fully in the employee manual. Check with your HR professional to assure these rules are up to date and implemented according to code and proper procedure as required in your area.

---

* A complete description of Values, Vision, Mission, and Message can be found in Glen Aubrey's book, *Leadership Is— How to Build Your Legacy.* Please visit www.LeadershipIs.com.

The next sections of PACE relate to performance standards in relationships and functions. The necessary accountability comprised within the objective views of the employee's contributions showcases both an employer's and employee's responsibilities, while the focus of the exercise remains the employee's relational and functional balance.

A statement of representation could be inserted at the beginning of this next section to help position this idea. For example, you may want to consider this sentence: "This account of your position and the evaluation of your contributions within it include two aspects of your performance: the decisions you make (relationships) and what you do (functions) that are associated and required with your job. These descriptions are not designed to be exhaustive and, with your full knowledge and at the discretion of your employer, may be modified from time to time, temporarily or permanently. Both employer and employee expect that additional tasks may be considered to be 'non-essential,' 'supplementary,' or 'auxiliary' to the primary focus points of your position. Employer and employee concur that these needs will be met within reasonable expectations and cooperation, based on full agreement. Employer and employee value contributions in primary and additional areas. Employer and employee see these to be parts of essential efforts in achieving balance in relationship and function."

<u>Relational Behaviors</u> (decisions about another's success)

Behaviors directly related to relationships (decisions) that the employee makes about other people's successes, whether on the core team on which the employee serves, or not connected to it, are listed first. Because relational behaviors represent 50% of an overall performance score, PACE should be designed to see whether relational behaviors contribute to the organization or division's Values, Vision, Mission and Message. The behaviors are weighed against a standard that requires they be demonstrated consistently. Weight with regard to scoring in these areas must equal 50% of the total score, as noted above.

It is strongly encouraged that the evaluator provides a comment when the employee's performance falls below or exceeds the agreed standard, designed to pinpoint specific areas of struggle or highlight significant degrees of success. Questions in this section are not designed to be answered "yes" or "no." Rather, they are presented in terms of discussion and degree.

Relational behaviors are applicable in an "across-the-board" spread, in that they can be used as the first half of nearly any job account and evaluation format. Relationships, because they are decisions, are more attitude- and choice-based, as opposed to functional- and duty-specific-based. The five groupings that follow are designed to provide descriptions that can and should be measured.

First represented are those relational behaviors that proactively support the quality and contribution improvement efforts. You may wish to modify them, but evaluation questions like these should be used. Samples:

1. How well does the employee recognize and pursue opportunities of customer care and participate in improving his or her quality of service to the customer?

2. How much does the employee request and encourage feedback from customers, vendors, and co-workers as to his or her dealings with them?

3. How well does the employee keep informed of important issues pertinent to the work place and its essential requirements?

4. What are some current examples of prevailing problems in this most recent reporting period that this employee has helped to solve, or positive issues he or she has helped to enhance?

Next, consider those behaviors that demonstrate a solid understanding of the worth and appropriate application of the employer and employee's resources. These can include, but not be limited to, materiel and personnel. In light of costs of acquisition, replacement, and the degree of commitment to assisting others with the use of these resources, they are evaluated in an open question format. Samples:

1. How well does the employee demonstrate flexibility and genuine willingness to support the organization's changing needs?

2. How efficiently does the employee maintain and allocate resources to promote efficient use of funds, energy and resources, assuring these are utilized effectively?

3. How important is the utilization of co-workers' ideas and actions that, when employed, help maximize output and minimize costs of operation?

4. How well does the employee manage time, including opportunities of working with other people, to help achieve fulfillment in their work-related tasks?

Third, relational behaviors will include demonstrations of professional and interpersonal commitment, care and communication skills. Samples:

1. To what degree does the employee demonstrate effective interpersonal skills and positive attitudes when interacting with clients or suppliers, applying the company's Values, Vision, Mission and Message into the interactions?
2. How well does the employee demonstrate respect, trust, and regard for other individuals, including varied cultural, emotional and informational needs of other team members, or outside clients or vendors?
3. How well does the employee illustrate genuine initiative in self-directed, responsive and courteous response and service to clients and others?
4. How important is communication to the employee, seen in presenting appropriate and complete information to co-workers, clients and vendors in a timely fashion? What is the description of "a timely fashion" to this employee?

Because the concept, concrete application, and implementation of core team solutions are vital elements in the study of *Industrial Strength Solutions*, the fourth description and evaluation centers on relational behaviors that proactively contribute to meet core team's goals. Samples:

1. To what degree does the employee actively demonstrate quality interpersonal skills and positive attitudes in interactions with team members and members of additional groups? How are these actions evidenced in support of Values, Vision, Mission and Message?
2. When new tasks or assignments are presented, how well does the employee demonstrate flexibility and a positive attitude toward their implementation and completion?

3. How well does the employee communicate appropriate information to customers, vendors and co-workers that is complete and consistent?

4. How much does the employee support the core team's or core team leader's decisions even though his or her views may differ?

5. To what extent does the employee illustrate effective team spirit and teamwork to accomplish core team and department's goals?

Finally, under relational behaviors, PACE should be formed to look for and evaluate behaviors that clearly demonstrate dependability, faithfulness and high accountability. Every core team member, for the success of the team to become reality, must commit to executing these in a consistent mode and model. Samples:

1. How willingly and consistently does the employee demonstrate compliance with the organization's standards for use of time and consistent attendance?

2. How well and often does this employee's commitment to punctuality demonstrate a dedication to helping others succeed?

3. How dedicated is the employee's agreement with, and conformance to, the vacation policy, seen in providing advance notification and planning, and a personal commitment to achieving balance and rest?

4. How well does the employee demonstrate flexibility in scheduling working hours and days that help meet needs of the departmental unit or core team, even if these exceed minimum requirements?

Measurement of Relational Behaviors

Measurement of relational attitudes and actions can be determined in many ways. Here are 14 ideas and samples of measurement. These sentences should be weighed, and a numerical score, letter grade, or other evaluation applied to each. Samples:

1. Customer comments and feedback support the employee's positive contributions.
2. Vendor comments and feedback reflect positive attitudes the employee presents.
3. On-time attendance and active participation in core team meetings are regular factors of engagement.
4. Respect for the members of the core team produces appropriate deference to, and support of, other people's contributions.
5. Respect for the members of other teams, supervisors, and subordinates demonstrate genuine desires for cooperation and completion.
6. Accomplishment of tasks ahead of time, where expectations in excellence of contribution and effect are exceeded, is a hallmark.
7. Feedback from the employee comes in concise formats that show respect for other people's characters, opinions and time.
8. Attitudes of promoting an individual, even though disagreeing with a position that individual is taking, are seen openly.
9. Initiatives in participation within conflict resolution procedures that require supervisor or manager intervention occur no more than twice in a reporting period. Inter-relational issues solved without supervisor intervention is regular. Employee has a solution-oriented mind-set.
10. Regular communication to a supervisor of completion of assigned tasks is a part of job fulfillment and a common factor of the employee's contributions.
11. Respect from the core team on which the employee serves, a natural evidence of commitment to high cooperation, is seen regularly.

12. Growth in leadership impact, influence and investment possibilities and participation are parts of the ongoing considerations of this employee, evidenced in desires to help others, and in building personal destiny and legacy. This employee openly encourages the development of others while trying earnestly to improve.
13. Affirmation comes from supervisors, and is received and shared with others on the core team, or other teams.
14. Encouragement to see others improve permeates the working atmosphere surrounding this individual.

Functional Behaviors (those actions that corroborate relational decisions)

There is no separation between relational and functional aspects of a person's contribution; one gives birth to the other, and relationships are always the parents, as has been shown. In noting and evaluating functional behaviors, both employer and employee should be keenly aware of how tasks and their completion fit in with, and contribute to, the organization or core team's goals, those operational mandates that constitute its mission. As with relational behaviors, functional behaviors represent 50% of an overall performance score, so PACE is crafted to assure that functional behaviors contribute to the organization or core team's overall Values, Vision, Mission and Message, and that they can be evaluated accordingly.

Behaviors in function are weighed against a standard of positional description that requires consistent demonstration. Areas of evaluation are listed as statements, not questions. Functional behaviors are related to accuracy, time, completeness, efficiency and excellence. Comments highlight specifics of accomplishment, and the evaluator's responsibility is to assign a score to each area in accordance with the measurement parameters set for the exercise. As with relational behaviors, the evaluator must comment as to areas of impediment that need improvement, noting specifics, or compliment successes, detailing particulars, where any job contribution dips beneath or exceeds agreed criteria.

An example is provided below. The behaviors noted are those inherent in an administrative or administration director's role. Obviously, behaviors for a particular job or position in your company must be altered according to specific duty requirements your positions demand. Your design will accurately reflect the position's qualifications and corresponding degrees of fulfillment.

In this example, PACE will consider this administrator's overall tasks and to what degree these are completed in a timely, consistent and professional manner. Let's assume for this presentation that the administrator of this core team or department unit has responsibilities for team member's time cards, budgetary record keeping, including invoicing to a select customer base, whether internal or external. Samples:

1. Employee performs tasks in a professional and timely practice with appropriate closure and communication to parties involved with, or connected to, task completion.
2. Employee's accuracy of processing time cards, record keeping, and preparing invoicing meets or exceeds standards.
3. Turn around time of accomplishing assignments is faithfully honored.
4. Employee completes and inspects his or her own work to assure accuracy before presentation or distribution.
5. Employee's contributions excel in attention to, and completion of, details.

An administration employee is destined to communicate with peers and other parties with whom the employee shares accountability. Therefore, the next PACE section should deal with the creation, implementation and continued maintenance of concise and clear communication paths with core team, other teams, clientele and vendors. Samples:

1. Employee establishes and sustains accurate dissemination of appropriate information through documents such as work and purchase orders, service requests, flow charts and job forms, implementing closure of tasks.
2. In an effort to satisfy or exceed the requirements of solid customer satisfaction, the employee provides accurate and complete information to internal or external clients and vendors, obtaining core team agreement and/or leadership's approval if requested or required.
3. Employee communicates accurate and succinct information regarding proper work functions to teams and leadership through communication vehicles most appropriate to this requirement, including, but not limited to, in-person, email, by phone or voice mail.
4. Employee pro-actively initiates contact with clients and vendors to establish new, and strengthen existing, networking relationships, accenting customer service with excellence and high accountability.
5. Employee responds graciously and with timely efficiency to client, core team and vendor questions and comments, and assures that communication loops are fully closed and associated actions are completely satisfied.

Because a description of contributions for any job cannot cover all the functional aspects of its workflow, a part of functional behavior must focus on supplemental or auxiliary duties and how well they are fulfilled. In our consultation services through Creative Team Resources Group, Inc., www.ctrg.com, we often state that the degree of excellence shown in the completion of extra curricular duties is a sure indicator of an employee's desire to obliterate mediocrity and transcend the "norm." Further, that true character is seen more in the completion of the additional than in the perfunctory accomplishment of the required. Along with explicit standards of performance of an employee's job requirements for which the employee is paid, the "above and beyond" contributions say even more about dedication and commitment. The PACE document should help the employee and reviewer establish how much and to what degree "normal" is surpassed.

This kind of perspective, of course, begins with the employee's decision to concentrate on more than just his or her area of responsibility, with an eye toward helping whenever and wherever needed, while still fulfilling job duties beyond the described requirements for meeting expectations. Samples:

1. In addition to performing required positional duties, the employee adopts an "overview" mindset, aware of the activities and affairs outside his or her immediate positional area, and is dedicated to assisting wherever needs arise, while fulfilling assigned tasks with excellence.
2. To assure that additional function is completed and communicated thoroughly, the employee maintains accurate archives and records of facts for appropriate and approved presentations to networking partners, those who may need this specific knowledge to enhance greater productivity.
3. Employee willingly engages in training, coaching and interactive learning with the core team or, as assigned, to other teams.
4. Because cooperation is valued and exercised, the employee provides assistance to other members of the organization within parameters of agreed, understood and reasonable expectations.

Measurement of Functional Behaviors

The PACE measurement of functional behaviors has its own list of guidelines and mile markers. Phrased in the form of questions, these should be answered "yes" or "no" and will often require explanations or proofs. Samples:

1. Are assignments or positional duties completed on time or ahead of time?

2. Do the contributions bring more than pecuniary value to the organization?
3. Does the employee earn for the company more than it costs the company to retain the employee in hard dollars?
4. Do the employee-generated profits produce five times the cost of retention or production? What are the bottom line comparative figures that prove this answer?
5. Are customers with whom the employee deals satisfied in the quality of the provision, and how do we know?
6. Are vendors with whom the employee has contact eager to do business with the company or organization because of the employee's demeanor and professionalism?
7. Is the employee receiving proper rewards commensurate with merit? What is the time line for a review of rewards?
8. Is appreciation noted in tangible ways: cards, letters, calls, messages, money, and is it freely received?
9. Does employee set time aside for specific training for new tasks?
10. Does employee welcome new components to help accomplish more in less time and with more efficiency?
11. Are expectations as to time lines for completion of job assignments acceptable, are they reached, and can they be exceeded?
12. Is attending to details producing greater quality behind the scenes?
13. Are conversations behind member's backs, or out of their hearing, uplifting and complimentary?
14. Is conflict resolution, where the parties concerned are the parties involved, a regular occurrence and producing beneficial results, and what part does employee play in this manifestation?

True character is seen more in the completion of the additional than in the perfunctory accomplishment of the required.

One of the keys to understanding the elements of mixing well is that the cooperative nature of relationships and functions is never dependent on feelings, although it can and will often include them. The power-force behind effective functioning is the strength of the decisions based on inherent good character and earnest desire. Feelings may or may not follow; regardless, they are a product, not a cause.

Or, another way of looking at this—functional behaviors are inherently tied to mental and physical appropriation of planning, expenditures of energy, time, activity, and just plain hard work coming from solid choices. Therefore, because achievements are direct results of sound decisions, questions regarding them can certainly be "yes" or "no" interrogatories. Explanations in support of the answers are correctly classified as welcomed additions in an atmosphere of encouragement, certainly not to be perceived as threats which cause defense mechanisms to kick in and take over.

Tangibles and Intangibles

Strong work efforts produce *tangibles,* hands-on results that are measurable, often seen in items bought and sold, or in the acquisition of, or the ability to acquire, things. Tangibles can also include pecuniary provisioning that permits and encourages monetary investment and growth over time. Tangible results are cumulative, and will be evidenced in lists of acquisitions and activities stimulated by the capacity of earned rewards.

In contrast, relational behaviors usually cannot be measured in tangibles; rather, they are constitutionally part of a category called *intangibles,* defined as those things which cannot be bought or sold, but, instead, are natural and inherent to character, and values-descriptive. These are traits like assurance, hope, integrity, consistency, professionalism, mutual respect, dignity, cooperation, love, confidence, truthfulness and fairness. The questions regarding effectiveness of relational behaviors are often phrased as open-ended discussion items, designed to delve into reasons behind function, focusing on beneath-the-surface issues instead of incidents alone, for within issues is where intangibles dwell.

The mixing of the elements of positional perspectives, personnel placements, and performance procedures should graphically showcase balance in relationship and function, intangible and tangible, if done correctly.

A Summary of PACE

In the development of PACE, provide sufficient space for an evaluator and employee's comments. These comments should be seen by both participants. Instructions regarding comments should emphasize that the comments should consist of forthright and succinct statements. Providing great comments is part of the learning experience that should attend the use of PACE, learning what to say and how to say it. This part of the process of the evaluation for employee and reviewer can be as important as the end result of the completion and scoring of the form, if not more so.

PACE should include a grid or spaces for notes and steps where the employee and employer together determine specific action plans designed to maintain, improve and/or quantitatively optimize an employee's work potential and job contribution. These action items are to be specific to the employee's work paradigms discovered and discussed in the document and the evaluation session. Specific action steps to be taken by *both* the supervisor and the employee are indicated and ratified in agreement. *It is vital that both participate in some level of action for accomplishment and endurance of required results.*

Further, time frames on each specific action item are placed on a calendar to aid in assessing progress and to provide needed accountability. Finally, you may wish to include this sentence on your PACE document: *"An action plan is required if the employee receives a work performance score of less than acceptable, beneath 'average,' or it is clearly shown that a fundamental imbalance exists between relationship and function from an overall point of view."* Set your PACE in place, and proceed.

The Elements of Mixing Well
Building Industrial Strength Solutions

Positional Perspectives	Personnel Placements	Performance Procedures
Designing and agreeing on what you want before you start	Correctly aligning the person and task, deed and need	Intentionally aligning the best people for best deliverables

Power Centers

Some people choose to dwell and work in shallow relationships. Perhaps living in these arrangements is perceived as less threatening, more comfortable and less risk-oriented. Surface-only relations are evidenced when the timid and intimidated wholly lean on others who appear stronger. The leaning folks probably hazard little, and may contribute virtually nothing as the more aggressive folks take the lead, brave the fall, or gain the win. Dedicated followers who desire to learn by proper association are not described here. This "lean" reference is to people who align with power for protection, and who desire this alignment to assure their own welfare with little or no regard to the success of anyone other than themselves.

These individuals attach themselves to power centers hoping that in that association may rest their security, both in feeling and placement. This is a sorry state of perceived strength at best and is strictly conditional because it is determined mainly by proximity to someone else's authority or image, occupying a place for face-saving, but only for a time. Strength may be assumed or even assured on the surface, but in the long run, a person who clings may become severely disappointed and further disenchanted if the power center shifts its attention or dissolves away all together.

People who seek proximity to power centers engage in temporary warmth and well-being of domination-by-cluster. They may project superiority complexes that in truth they don't really possess at all. A common misunderstanding is this: that the person who is in the know because they touch the center of authority today, is the person who will be the last to go tomorrow if the changes come to stay. Not always. In consideration of building industrial strength solutions, power centers seldom ever exist where "free riders" are allowed free reign or even a meager existence, not to mention any assurance of a non-threatened future. Proximity to power centers exists where manipulative maneuvering is the goal. It demonstrates the antithesis of personal responsibility, values-driven contributions and innovation, and avoids team cooperation. Proper alignment of relationship and function cannot coexist where proximity to power is of central importance.

One of the most insidious strains of personnel dysfunction—where desire and manipulation for power center placement is present and competition for the corner offices fierce—is the misinformed and imagined allegiance demanded by insecure leaders who exercise misplaced authority from a position they never earned, or from the vacuum of lessons they never learned. Their theory is that if they can align with a power center long enough it will guarantee their futures, and they may care less how their juxtaposition may affect others who practice more genuine intent to grow and mature without leeching strength from somebody else.

What these misaligned folks really create is a state of being tied to little more than the whims of change, and when the changes come they may simply be discarded. Alternatively, where relationships matter more than position and security is based more on shared values instead of manipulation for status, this "need" for proximity to "the top" simply assumes far less importance, or diminishes and evaporates all together. Desires for power center positioning assuredly fade when confronted with building truth-based strong relationships and corroborating functions, because secure core team members stand on their convictions and embrace uplifting cooperation, refusing to hide behind someone else's skirts or successes.

How close to a power center do you think you need to be, and for what reason? Or, do you believe you need to actually be the power center? The closer to a power center one feels is necessary for comfort, likely the more insecure and less valuable that person really believes he or she is in personal worth and strength of character. The loss can be monumental for those who have placed inflated worth on positional strength when the influence that made them is removed, and they are no longer part of a counterfeit attachment. If a position of power has been the most prominent determining factor of perceived effectiveness, then that effectiveness is relegated to being a mere charade when it is ultimately exposed for its true composition.

Truly powerful people, where power is seen as a tool to benefit and not to destroy, don't require titles or positions as motivators or causes for excellence, nor do they have the need for close proximity to powerful cloisters to know acceptance and worth. Instead, they are secure enough to know they are valuable, regardless. In point of fact, truly powerful people exercise humility because it is a part of their true essence, and in that exercise they generate power! Their words and actions prove their true security and dedication, no matter the title or place. Leaders, bosses, and others of influence will often come to the confident person for advice, counsel, perspective, and requests for involvement, because within that confident person resides character that outshines the evasiveness of comfortable privilege.

In short, true power seeks out competent and complete people, those who don't have to seek after a position of supremacy or alignment to prove their worth. Their faithfulness and commitment are rewarded because their power comes from within, not from without. Their true and stellar contributions are honored because they are results of good choices, and these people and their choices often change their surroundings. People who contribute from character as opposed to control stand out in reputation because they create it.

Strength, as a condition or state of being, doesn't just happen; it is a result of intentional positioning of people, positions, priorities, places, and perspectives. In this understanding strength is not conditional, that is, moved by circumstance or winds of temporary change. Rather, strength is a visible result, born of desire and action, implemented in growing and healthy relationships, founded on agreements of values and the decisions for action that accompany them.

A core team's functions prove the endurance of the relational commitments their members make as they contribute within workable solutions. They are working well, out of strength, learned and earned, not contrived or connived, and certainly not improperly aligned. Position Account and Contribution Evaluation exercises help leaders and team members live in relational and functional balance, and power centers are replaced with contributions coming from character, regardless of position, title or tenure.

Creating industrial strength solutions is an engagement of people in combination with their work. To be accomplished well, certain attributes should be identified as both those to which a core team strives, and those against which measurements of its successes can be made. We will turn to consider these attributes now.

Chapter 7:
Attributes of Industrial
Strength Solutions

The Walled City

Imagine a formidable and thickly walled city of antiquity, set on a gently rising hill. It is home to several thousands of people who constitute their own kingdom. They are for the most part self-sufficient, with gardens, livestock and stables, merchants and local hand-crafted manufacturing, and an interior spring that provides the water they need.

The high walls of stone surrounding this city are themselves encircled by a deep moat stretching the length of its outside perimeter, fed by the spring. Each of its six gates is heavily guarded against intrusion, crossing the moat is only possible by boat, and these crafts are kept ever at the ready on the city-side of the water.

In addition to its population, the city is home to vast treasures, a fact known to many of its inhabitants as well as foreigners far and wide. For its protection, the city possesses a well-equipped and finely trained army—superior for its day. This army is ever on alert. Their troops are keenly jealous of their kingdom and what it represents. Their vigilance is high, and for good reason. This city's treasures are worth several kings' ransoms and would be a prize for any enemy. Because it is so well-endowed, its enemies abound, and often seek to threaten its security.

Generally the populace lives at peace, however. They feel secure. They have seldom been attacked, and never once has any attack succeeded. It is true, that of the enemies that have approached to plunder and destroy, some have reached to within the proximity of a day's hard ride, but outposts manned with squads of soldiers and riders have engaged the enemy on neutral turf, sending swift couriers to warn the city as they have held the enemy at bay. When engaged, these couriers approach the city quickly, and with known signals and sounds of horns, alert the watchmen who are on the city's walls. The watchmen respond—they blow their trumpets long and loud. Their trumpet blasts warn the citizenry, and at the same time become the summons for the home army and its riders to bolt into action. Horses and riders, footmen and archers assemble promptly, and those who are needed outside the city walls are quickly ferried across the moat, deployed as an offensive force. If the coordinated response mechanisms work well, then before an enemy can make its advance upon the city and its valuable possessions, the home army rides out to meet the attackers head-on. A large contingent of heavily armed troops remains within and upon the walls to guard the homeland itself should the enemy succeed in conquering the city's defenders who have taken the offense.

Indeed, for an enemy who wishes to conquer this city, several obstacles would have to be overcome. First, the heavily guarded outposts would need to be overrun. The couriers would have to be intercepted before they reached the city to alert the watchmen. And if these goals could be achieved, a force of an exceptionally grander size would be needed to cross the moat and take the walls. Only through stealth, surprise and trickery would any of this become possible.

Conquering this city, in an enemy's view, was no small task, and had never been fulfilled. Until one day an enemy, through the trickery of a false alliance, and by sheer force of numbers and stealth of night, overran an outpost, killing all its couriers except one who was captured for the treachery to come. Unimpeded, this enemy advanced, and the city was completely unaware.

In the dead of night a watchman on the wall noticed a flickering light—one that he had never seen before. He was instantaneously alert, wondering what this was and what it could mean. His eyes strained to see, his ears to hear. The wind was strong, masking other sounds, and the light evaporated in mists to become darkness once again. Still, he was suspect, and looked and listened hard, straining with every breath to determine the cause of the flicker that was no more. It was then he heard a familiar voice and saw the signal of two flaming arrows with which he was familiar. The voice had uttered the key words—and he had answered, and breathed easier. It was a known courier, checking in.

But, in fact, these calls had come from the courier who had been captured, who was forced to address the watchman with known signs of assurance. This watchman, unaware of the incredible danger that lurked just beyond his realization, took what he knew to be familiar as a reasonable assurance that all was well. But his ignorance could not forestall looming misfortune that lurked and advanced.

Because the watchman was misinformed, the alarm to the citizenry and their protectors remained mute. Having constructed small boats to be carried on their shoulders, the enemy ferried their warriors across the moat. Again the captured courier called to the watchman, who, upon recognition of the "all is well" signal, authorized the opening of the gates. The city had dwelt for a brief time in a false security, and when the attack commenced the devastation and plundering was total. It was too late before anyone could stop the onslaught they had unwittingly permitted. Obliterating everything in its path, having no regard for those who were soldier or civilian, the city was caught in a murderous wave of destruction, its rulers killed, its population enslaved, its treasures seized. This domain of antiquity was literally wiped from the face of the earth, never to rise again.

The watchman didn't sound the trumpet because, according to his sense of the condition at the time, all was secure. Although he was wary, he was falsely assured, and desperately misinformed. Total devastation resulted even as prepared as the city thought it was. The enemy had come upon them in ways they had not known, and won the day.

Few enjoy a story with an unhappy ending, unless in support of the evil conqueror. But this illustration is presented because it represents many of the uninformed and complacent attitudes that pervade current business climates and endeavors. The enemy in the story may not necessarily represent outside competition within similar industries. More often it will symbolize severe internal distractions: behind-the-back disagreements in decisions, faulty or non-existent communication, misaligned standards, misguided motivations, manipulation, intimidation, insubordination, and other destroyers of team success.

Insidious internal pressures can weigh heavily on commerce and the teams who try to conduct business better. Some of these negative impulses originate from deviant people who willfully violate core values, promoting and displaying attitudes and actions that test structures germane to an organization's true advantage of great character. Organizations that are founded upon values, uplifting beliefs, superior causes, and agreements in proven principle must be aware, and battle this insidiousness non-stop, whenever and wherever it occurs. They will war against the jealously, envy, distrust, inadequate or absent conclusions, and insufficient and therefore ineffective communication that, if permitted, will undermine their existence. Too many assumptions, an absence of facts, a lack of openness and too much gossip—all of these encroach and foster reproach if allowed to go unchecked. The core team that functions well recognizes that the temptation to tolerate or endure them is ever present. They are the enemy within. So a great team checks and destroys them.

The "watchmen" for the teams are those people in an organization who are consistently on the alert for the disruption that would forestall a group's effectiveness and waylay its production. These watchmen may be supervisors, team leaders, those with influence and authority, or they may be people of impact and influence who take responsibility seriously, regardless of position or title. They rely, and should, on other responsible people who possess information as to problems foreseen and ways to meet problems head-on. If a formidable challenge to an organization's health and security becomes apparent, and its leader or influence people are not aware, an entire organization can suffer, and chaos can result.

One of the responsibilities of a team leader or influence person is to sound the alarm when a danger becomes known. Knowledge about the danger and of what it is made is often dependent on the quality, quantity and timeliness of the information a responsible party has coming to him or her. If faulty, a false alarm may be the result. If accurate, then an alert will call the teams to action, and at that moment a great offense can be its best defense.

Intriguingly, when a warning is sounded, the watchman, or leader/influencer, is absolutely not in charge of the responses of his or her followers, even though he or she may wish they were. For while the watchman can try to demand, his or her primary job is to warn and tell the truth, helping to position the people to best confront an invader because accurate communication has been presented and heard. A leader's command effectiveness is to be seen in the allegiance the core team people pay to the warning and the quality of the execution of an offensive plan because it has been rehearsed well. The watchman, this leader, shall never leave his or her post of responsibility, even when the action of confrontation gets thick. You see, the leader may be needed in that position of responsibility for the next onslaught that is sure to follow. Preparation is not sacrificed on an altar of urgency, if this team is ready.

The illustration reveals that what a supervisor or manager brings to the table has been thoroughly analyzed and tested, reliable and proven. For this watchman on the wall, his or her take on a situation is critical, and his or her response, to sound the alert or not to call others to action, is crucial. For those in the field who are best positioned to let leaders know what is ahead, their responsibilities for communicating accurate information are vital to life and success.

Consider this: when a provisional source within a structure breaks down, ceases to communicate or gives faulty information, how will the watchman know that the time may be "now" to sound the alarm? Further, if the alarm is not heralded appropriately or in time, what may the outcome be? What could occur if the watchman, for whatever reason, leaves or abandons the post? What are the results when the responses of those within the group reflect little or no serious consideration of the warnings presented, and inaction is chosen because they don't care, or "have heard it all before?" Unfortunately, these kinds of scenarios, in varying forms, characterize the activities of business groups, teams, organized units, and entire companies far too frequently, especially in times of challenge. The reasons for this dysfunction, when analyzed fully, time and again point to effusive failures in applying four critical areas of relationships and operational functionality. These critical areas are called Four Attributes of Industrial Strength Solutions. They are: Holistic View, Wholeness, Humility and Firm Resolve. These are fully explained below.

Thankfully, when these four attributes are chosen, affirmed and applied, the channels of communication for proper information open wide and are eagerly sought. Communication becomes more effective: what is expected is what is given, what is given is what is received, and what is exchanged in the transaction becomes the foundation of appropriate and diligent action.

When these four attributes are fully engaged, the response is far less re-action and more pro-action, based on declared desire instead of detouring defense. When energetically employed, the people of a core team become attuned, fully aware, wary of negative situations, and poised to implement good works through the application of the attributes. There is no doubt about the merits of this interaction.

These four attributes and their actions are necessary to the very existence and extension of an organization of strength. Indeed, they are the ingredients of choice in creating workable solutions that withstand tempest, temptation, trial, and test. Each core team or group member chooses these, born of mutual desires for success, where all share in the security and all work to assure its permanence. In healthy groups, each member adopts and fully utilizes these attributes consistently.

The attributes are powerful characteristics of winners, not whiners. They are hard to achieve, but because they appear so simple to understand, their complexity of character baffles the proud and gives strength to those who would be willing to take up their precedence. They require firm commitment if one chooses them, dedicated diligence in their pursuit, and forgiveness when people falter in their efforts to enact them.

These four attributes are commanding, compelling, comprehensive, and deeply missed when they are absent. In fact, when any of them are not present, the team suffers.

Core teams who desire best decisions based on solid standards, who are continually motivated to achieve their goals, and who want to empower group members to win, lead, supervise and follow well, will choose these four attributes as essential ingredients to the mix of the workable solutions which they form, and out of which they function. Here are their definitions:

1. Holistic View: The perspective coming from the desire to see the bigger picture, seeking understanding from

multiple sources and sifting information to delineate appropriate action

2. <u>Wholeness</u>: A state of being characterized by living at peace with one's self and living in viable and growing relationships with others, where agreement on values is the foundation for interchange and cooperation

3. <u>Humility</u>: A characteristic of character coming from the choice to prefer others before self, placing their agendas first, giving freely from one's own storehouse to assure opportunities of success

4. <u>Firm Resolve</u>: Declared and unwavering commitment to action, where success aligns with true values and motives, and methods exemplify an unalterable dedication to living and working in truth

Each requires careful examination. Each is a choice, and is a choice ingredient of industrial strengths. Industrial strength solutions that last beyond the resolution of an immediate need are enlivened when these four are present, activated, and cooperating—no easy task in a competitive business climate where fast is seen to be preferred over fine, and where the expectation and realization of customers receiving great product and service may be the exception and not the rule.

So let's explore their constitution and implementation in the workplace that values people first and where enhanced function follows.

<u>Holistic View:</u>

A vision of the bigger picture allows a core team member a number of advantages. Among them are these:
- Appropriate information to allow proper functioning
- Seeing the worth of an individual's participation in relation to the importance of the overall goal
- Comprehension of how an individual's contributions fit

and advance group achievement, a recognition of how collective contributions enhance overall health

- Delineation of appropriate action at right times and in right places, reinforcing weaker areas with stronger elements
- Transfer of ownership of duties when appropriate to those who are more equipped to handle them
- The creation of team cooperation, as fulfillment of one responsibility prepares the way for completion of another

Segmented views, especially where the right hand does not know what the left hand is doing—and should know—produce disjointed "do's" and obviously represent disconnect. Characteristics of segmentation include: frustrated communication and burdened people, when procedures are forced to change at the last minute because one person didn't plan well or even at all, didn't inform the team, didn't fulfill a required function, didn't come through on time, forgot, didn't care, left loops unclosed, promised action that was never intended to have commensurate delivery, and through these inconsiderate gestures produced havoc and falling domino effects. To correct these problems a lot of un-doing usually becomes necessary, more energy has to be expended, not to mention time and money, and a general, haphazard "picking up" of the pieces that hopefully may be reassembled.

Holistic viewing requires diligent efforts to glean information from right sources to form solid understandings of a consistent whole, much like the jigsaw puzzle that requires a glance if not a study of the photo example of what to expect when all the pieces are in place, before the assembly begins. Acquisition of needful information is a primary responsibility of a core team leader when decisions as to allocation of resources and commensurate actions are contemplated. Bottom line, the leader needs to ask the necessary questions of the people who have the proper information, or retrieve it from storage sources, or better yet, receive it from people who proactively seek to inform. These people empower that leader to make good decisions—those choices that will have a strong bearing on the accuracy and fulfillment of final outcomes.

Evaluating information, deciding what to keep and apply, or to dismantle and discard, is a stage of judgment in a process of prioritization where outlines of actions and their required timelines are determined. Sifting information, as part of a production process, is as important as serving no wine "before its time." Prioritization of great information, acquired from legitimate and trustworthy sources, allows a team to know that the job at hand is organized. Prioritization shows what is important, why, when it will be accomplished, by whom, and who will benefit. Further, the team understands how its actions will contribute to proper utilization of time, money, personnel and energy resources, and produce the efficiency their workable solution should demand.

The importance of a holistic view as a positive attribute of building industrial strength solutions is readily seen. The challenge, of course, is to take the necessary effort to grasp the view, re-view it as often as necessary, and then act on what the true view says. It's all in the acquisition, action and appropriate alignment of good information. As projects and respective duties are assigned, they are fully understood, valued, communicated, completed and their communication loops closed when the project is fulfilled.

Wholeness:

As defined above, wholeness is a state of being that originates from living at peace with one's self, and growing with others in solid relationships characterized by shared core values. Living at peace with one's self is possible if integrity is present. Enjoying shared relationships requires this integrity, too. But where integrity is wanting, desires to avoid responsibility emerge, walls are built for isolation, truth telling is rare or non-existent, and a refusal exists to confront issues that beg for resolution. Certainly cooperation is absent from anyone so positioned.

Wholeness is a human condition for which an honest person craves, and that longing, if deep enough, will motivate dedicated efforts and hard work to walk through negative experiences, not shrink from their challenges. Wholeness will patch up torn relationships through forgiveness and grace, and seek common grounds of cooperation because values have been realigned. It is through these efforts that peace has its best opportunity to appear and remain.

Internal peace is not born of hermitage, nor does it dwell in conflict avoidance. Nor is it generally seen or appreciated when life is full and things are going well.

This truth may appear to be just incredulous, but real and lasting peace is more readily evident when life is tough, where the rough and tumultuous moments toss and wound, and where character, diligence, dedication and resolve stand firm against the tests of the immediate, and overcome the harsh impediments of the past. Real peace is a condition where the person who seeks to conquer engages in the conflict, fights for right and sees that values that are tested remain true. Real peace is that posture where the hero emerges better for the trials, and is empowered to confront his or her own futures with fortitude and confidence. Real peace, for one who wins, becomes an atmosphere of earned security where the conqueror reaches and teaches others who suffer, or are preparing to confront similar difficulties, showing them through example how to endure, learn, grow, mature and move on. Real peace comes when the process of winning has beaten down overwhelming odds and the goals have been surely won.

The Three Artists

Three artists were asked to compete in a contest to see which of them could most accurately depict an abstract theme on canvas. The theme chosen for the contest was "peace." A substantial amount of money was the prize for the artist who best painted the portrait of this concept, so each diligently set about to apply sketches and colors to depict what he or she imagined "peace" would be.

The first artist painted a scene of a quiet Kansas corn field, fluffy clouds lazily meandering through their journeys underneath a blue-skied canopy, a silo with its barn and country home nestled amid plentiful crops, while rolling fields touched by gentle winds dissolved onto distant horizons, and delicate birds aloft circled aimlessly. It spoke of the serenity of a quiet summer's afternoon, idyllic, undisturbed by man or episode.

The second artist through his palette crafted the interior of a grand European cathedral where gently fashioned luminary arrays filtered down with holy solemnity, bidding their gentle beams float softly through stained glass mists, rugged wooden pews that beckoned of solitude and sacred petition, candles' flames alive, delicately flickering in honor of the holy. It was a hushed reverence this environment commanded where not a person could be seen or heard.

The third artist, challenged by this concept, willing to risk, and encouraged by his years of experience and fortitude, developed a canvass where at once immeasurable and immediate violence reigned and danger resounded—he painted an awful storm at sea. Waves fomented their relentless wrath, formed and crashed, pitched and rolled in thundering and enduring fury upon a cragged and forbidding shore that told of eons of unmitigated power thrust upon its throne, beaten and worn down through countless millennia from the savagery of the unsettled, unpredictable and war-destructive power of bursting water. One could almost hear the deafening anger-roars as the brine

INDUSTRIAL STRENGTH SOLUTIONS

reached again and again to reclaim what it took to be hers.

An observer of this work, gazing upon this conflict, breathed anew, sighing, gratefully relieved that this location was far from where he or she would ever like to be. Until a new scene, unveiled in the corner and almost imperceptible, just in the allure of intrigue, beckoned the eye. Amidst the foam and restless serums, underneath emboldened outcroppings of rock, engulfed in security, sheltered from this storm's awful presents, was a seagull, snuggled in its own repose, warm, dry, and at rest. It was waiting beneath layers of ravished stones for another tumult to spend its fury so its unimpeded flight could resume, abiding until the moment when it would once more soar aloft of all. For this creature, severe ravages of momentary discomfiture did not bother its gentle rest, for she was safe in the surrounding coves. Perhaps instinctively, regardless, it was true: apart from these clefts that sheltered it, it would surely have been dashed to its death within the storms that had come before.

There was no doubt which artist won the contest.

The third artist won the contest because the picture portrayed a steadfast premise: it is in the unsettled times that peace is known if security is sure. When turmoil invades experience it is then that peace can be a dwelling place for a time, as assurance displaces doubt. Peace is that state of quiet and monumental endurance where shelter and protection are revealed through enduring belief, eternal values, confidence and grounded hopes. Peace proclaims that what is experienced now shall not only pass, but the person pushing through the tumult will become better because of it. So, press on.

Living at peace with one's self is the beginning of a capacity and capability to dwell in, and contribute to, the viable and growing relationships with others who share like values and perspectives, or who desire to learn them because they are evidenced as true lessons of life. These are the lessons worth learning and retaining.

Agreement on a mutually shared value system* is a foundation upon which solid relationships can be constructed. Further, this agreement is the doorway to a healthy interchange of viewpoints, even promotion of discussion where parties disagree and conflict resolution is practiced, so that cooperation on the essentials is the result. Where one lives in this kind of wholeness, or earnestly desires it, that person will more willfully assume responsibility of his or her mistakes, learn from them, and contribute to others who may face similar challenges. Wholeness is the position where the experience has been permitted to be the teacher, and the student was humble enough to learn.

Combining team members who view wholeness as an attribute to be desired and acquired are inspired to communicate better, work together in healthier environments they help to create, and enjoy the freedom to produce excellence in their productivity. Wholeness is not a state of perfection, ever. It is, however, a state of strong desire for health, victory, learning, and contribution where people demand more of themselves than they do of others, and earnestly look for ways of contributing to other's successes, which in and of itself is the essence of strong relationships.

---

*You are encouraged to obtain and reference *Leadership Is-- How to Build Your Legacy* by Glen Aubrey (www.LeadershipIs.com) for a thorough explanation and sample of a Value System and the Nine Proofs upon which it is based and evaluated.

Humility:

Closely related to meekness, which is defined as strength under proper control, humility is the glue that holds relationships together because its central premise and focus is the welfare (good standing) of the other person in any helpful and right exchange. True humility permeates an atmosphere and is known where it exists. On a team, humility creates desires for improvement because no one selfishly clings to hoarded methods to protect their own agendas; rather, humble people are overtly open to new ways and willingly submit to recommendations for action shown to be more advantageous than what they may be doing currently.

Trumpeting humility is of course an oxymoron and incompatible with the true essence of the term and its application. A truly humble person thinks and acts less on behalf of him or her self, and more for the benefit of those who, in a team working environment, receive much from the inherent goodness and quality this kind of a decision brings. Humility is the essence of strong relationships shown by the decisions one makes about another's success, verified in the actions that follow.

Think of some of the most giving people you know. If the worth of their giving transcends the giver's need to be recognized, especially by the recipients of the gifts, you are probably dealing with a person who is truly humble, or desires to be. One of the greatest books that dwells extensively on this kind of giving, its processes and the joys it brings, is *Dr. Hudson's Secret Journal* by Lloyd C. Douglas. It is a truly inspiring book, one that this author has read multiple times since childhood, and it ingeniously describes in story form the benefits of doing good deeds minus the fanfare. This book is strongly recommended.

Humility is a choice, not a gift, but its presence truly gives great gifts where no one cares who receives the credit, if the source of the credit can even be determined. The point is that the source is no longer important when the gift is freely presented from a heart-attitude that does not seek its own place or position of credit.

On a core team, humble people make each other's jobs easier and more effective and find great joy in helping others succeed. Strong evidences of humility in action are these:

- Preparations for job fulfillment are completed ahead of time and under budget.

- Follow-up to a proposal is anticipated and accomplished before its due date, and its information does not have to be chased down.
- Movement of personnel, materiel, or money is positioned from an attitude of assisting instead of a response from someone insisting.
- An agreed process is initiated and implemented, not impeded, when an enterprise is young, in formative stages, or nearing completion.
- Cooperation replaces unhealthy and destructive internal competition.
- Difficulties are dissolved before they rear their heads as problems to overcome.
- Fruits of combined labor dwell in creative innovation, instead of getting bogged down in the crushing frustration that comes when tasks are not finished and communication loops are left dangling, and blaming and naming are the methods employed for critiquing errors or misjudgments.

Humility replaces negatives with service attitudes and actions that build up and expect the greater good to be the result.

Humility is a demonstration of vast, monumental and probably immeasurable strengths under control. It exists to give itself away in gentle portions or in amounts equal to current needs so that others are the recipients of its disbursement, and win because of its receipt. In the process, the humble person wins as well, in the knowledge of good deeds, the excellence of provision, and a heightened contribution beyond expectation, whether or not anyone knows the "who," because if known, humility could be gone.

<u>Firm Resolve:</u>

Commitment to following through, closing loops in communication, excellence in task completion, and commensurate accountability in relationships are parts of an understanding of faithfulness as central to good character. Firm resolve does not exist without these traits.

Commitment becomes less than its name implies when it is sacrificed because of expediency or convenience. So this sacrifice is not considered. Excuses, whining, victimization and living in a charade of unrealistic or undeclared expectations cannot coexist within firm resolve.

Firm resolve includes the unwavering, immovable, rock solid dedication to agreed action, and settles for nothing less than full completion and closure. Closely related to authenticity and accountability, firm resolve is a demonstration in outward observance that an internal decision has merit, and that ideas, decisions, words and actions are cohesive elements of a completed whole. Completion is so tied to firm resolve that an unfinished task or unresolved issue become their own motivators toward closure for the core team who decides to work within authenticity.

Firm resolve is a characteristic of the outward working of principles (values, and a value system) where doubts are replaced with confidence—that if a commitment is made, it will be accomplished well. Core values upon which a resolved action is based are tried and true where they are shown to be authentic, and agreement from supporting parties is not optional if a commitment withstands negative influences that are bound to come.

Firm resolve lives in truth. Truth in deeds raises a faithfulness quotient and sets a standard. This standard places people in positions to decide if they want it or not. If they want it, their behaviors support that desire because principled truth seeks resolution and closure. And although people with firm resolve respect those who may not wish to participate, they never back up.

Firm resolve comes from a clear recognition of motives, the reasons "why" an enterprise is decided, and incorporates methods integrated with integrity of purpose, right and honorable action. Firm resolve interlocks principle, practice, procedure and the people who make it all come to pass.

Firm resolve provides the impetus for cooperating members not to be dissuaded from their goals or persuaded to compromise their intentions or integrity. Firm resolve bolsters the causes to which they are committed, transcends and gives fuller meaning to their daily contributions to fulfill them.

Firm resolve tells core team people they can count on one another because each is committed to faithfulness and finality, and to finishing well. Firm resolve is not dependent on payment or lack of it; it lives and is rewarded on higher planes that include payments in multiple forms, but may constitute its own rewards from earned dignity of jobs well done.

Four Attributes of Industrial Strength Solutions
The Chosen Ingredients

Holistic View	Wholeness	Humility	Firm Resolve
The perspective coming from the desire to see the bigger picture, seeking understanding from multiple sources and sifting information to delineate appropriate action.	A state of being characterized by living at peace with one's self, and living in viable and growing relationships with others, where agreement on values is the foundation for interchange and cooperation.	A characteristic of character coming from the choice to prefer others before self, placing their agendas first, giving freely from one's own storehouse to assure opportunities of success.	Declared and unwavering commitment to action, where success aligns with true values and motives, and methods exemplify an unalterable dedication to living and working in truth.

Remember, these four attributes are choices, none occur because of wishful thinking or hope ungrounded in desire and decisive action. These ingredients are chosen because when mixed together in a workable solution (the people of the core team) the combination of these ingredients produces a fusion greater in its consolidation than the individual elements would be in isolation from one another.

Leaders and followers eagerly seek to combine these choice ingredients into groups that desire relational health and heightened productivity. Your job as a core team participant, regardless of position or title, is to ascertain from others on your team if these elements are present, if the agreements exist on shared values. If "yes," then your responsibility is to creatively propose, if not spearhead, actions to match, mix and mature the composite result into a well-designed and directed group, stronger and more agile than before the mix occurred.

One of the core traits of a strong mix of people who provide industrial strength solutions, who live in and contribute to their chosen ingredients, is balance, evidenced in proper equilibrium and consistent ebb and flow of rest and work. Consideration of this vital determiner is our next destination.

Chapter 8:
Achieving Balance

Balance is a state of existence that, unfortunately, does not come naturally or coincidentally to groups or teams who strive and persevere toward excellence. In fact, balance may be a word that is mentioned seldom and, when it is brought up at all, quickly dismissed because its definition and application are foreign, maybe not preferred, and are rarely seen in practical experience. Certainly the word is common, but the exercise of what it means may require even more discipline than the dedication to achieving great people and production, although it should be integral to the process within healthy team mixtures.

Balance, for business and teams, is defined as a measured equilibrium that gauges and evaluates perspective and action against an agreed standard of health. It is the process of instituting and distributing unified weight and importance to more than one necessary element of a work mixture at the same time.

Creating industrial strength solutions that endure requires balance. The context for the term in this book refers to the unification and intentional positioning of work and rest, taking and making appropriate and needful times for both actions, to allow the cycles with which humans are born and required to embrace to transpire freely, uninhibited. Not driven by personality's whims or changes in circumstances, balance plays a central part in the life and work styles of a healthy individual who wants to contribute in a wholesome environment, consistently. Balance is achieved when people not only know their limits as to how much work they should engage, but how much rest is required for harmonized existence and contribution as well.

Physical, mental, emotional, and spiritual aspects of the core team members are combined and understood as indispensable if the members of a team want to achieve balance within themselves and as a group. None of the aspects are fully achieved without a networked relationship to the others. Parts of a whole person, they are inter-related and inter-dependent. What affects one, affects all.

Working beyond reasonable expectations, where an individual's holistic health is put at risk, is too high a price to pay for the imagined results that could be achieved. When a person's family, attitudinal, physical, mental, emotional, and spiritual well-being is set aside because of over-abundant pressures and perceived or real responsibilities, whole destruction can be the result over time. The person and team who want productive and happy people will proactively factor in balance between work and rest, they will plan for it, calendar it, promote, uphold and respect it, not allowing what is not needful to become the dictator of that which can be, and often is, harmful. Honoring the people who desire balance and removing the inhibitors to its manifestation are good actions that prove that the crucial element of balance is important to the integrated health of every member on the core team. When properly planned and included as an expectation of core team participation, balance promotes health and longevity, and ultimately provisions best opportunities for greater fulfillment of roles and contentment of the people who perform them.

Real business life says that when a team is facing deal lines and deadlines, balance-due financial statements, customer service requirements, shipping and receiving schedules, imposing calendars, over-committed supervisors' demands, tax audits and progress reports, putting balance on the table as an important and vital consideration can be difficult to achieve. Plus, "Type A"-driven folks are prone to think that rest and relaxation should happen only after the work is done, that R and R is only opportune when circumstances permit, or at that point when the "big" job is completed, regardless of the effort and expense to the people involved. Balance relegated to "when we get some time" or "when things slow down a bit" or "when the demands lessen up" is not prioritized correctly. Simply put, a perspective of positioning balance to convenience or circumstance is damaging, and wrong.

Consideration of an appropriate mixture of leisure, laughter, love and life, as well as purpose, plan, provision, and profit is needful, and is a hallmark of the quality combination of relationship (decisions) and function (tasks). Again, we are reminded that if it is true that people are more important than what they do, then a motive and move toward achieving balance is not really optional for a team who desires health and well-being as well as productivity and profit. In fact, if a team violates the principle of balance they will pay a price. But if they honor the principle, it pays them.

Balance for one may not be the same in execution as balance for another, of course. In a core team who desires "best people" and "best products" together, agreement must be obtained on what balance is in terms of actual calendaring and activity. And it must be deliberately decided, realistically defined, definitively calendared, and then, done! Work has a way of always being there, so unless specific times of rest or non-work "space" are provisioned, truly needed "away" moments may be excused or exorcised from a person's list of "To Do" items. Few more harmful excises are known.

Consider what balance is, in real terms. Try this method: to see what a trait is, look for what it is not. This comparison may help people focus on what balance can be when it is placed within the rhythm of life and work. So, let's view a partial list of the characteristics of the opposite of balance first, those of imbalance.

Imbalance

1. Is noted for efforts to place unrealistic expectations on selected aspects of a person's ability to contribute, while ignoring other and more important facets of their makeup.
2. Fosters motives and movements to over-excel at a payment of that which should never be sold, namely a person's overall well-being.
3. Hinders creative thinking and action because the person who is enmeshed in imbalance simply may be too tired, running on empty. No apparatus, especially a human one, can function for long without the fuel that comes from rest.
4. Promotes stress, frustration and lack of clear judgment, impairing good perspective because it is living in the expedient, robbing vitality.
5. Focuses energies unnaturally on actions that may not be essential to the main cause, creating busywork, neglecting the more important goals, substituting the "not as good" for the good.
6. Advances selfish ambition and, as a result, possesses little if any means or reserves "left over" to invest in another person.
7. Contributes to the onset of pain, and has little tolerance for its existence. This pain is often manifested in more than one area (physical, emotional, mental, spiritual), and imbalance offers little hope or understanding of how to cope with, or treat, the pain when it comes. Imbalance

promotes less than desirable methods of help and cure, including but not limited to the cover-ups of unhealthy or illegal addictions and other improper substitutes for methods of treatment, stimulating victimization.

8. Skews the ability to see proactive solutions and encourages feelings of despair or destitution when a person dwells in despondence or dives to a level of inappropriate dependence.

9. Builds walls that block understanding of relationships and corroborating function.

10. Stifles growth when two or more people have to come together to work on a project where alternatively, under a balanced situation, they would more likely compliment each other as they combined their efforts; in an unhealthy competition of imbalance their growth is hindered and they refuse to give or receive encouragement and instruction, building silos.

11. Contributes to breakdowns in communication, hasty and inaccurate conclusions that, if unchecked, can lead to destruction of character and failures of function.

12. Marks immature individuals who try to superimpose undue and unnecessary requirements on other team members, inhibiting maturity and development, fostering discordance.

13. Attacks and criticizes those who wish to become stable in relationship and function, constricting growth, imposing artificial limits on what is good to fulfill the misaligned desires of selfish ambition.

The picture this list and its descriptions paint is all too common in the contemporary work world. In contrast, contributing within industrial strength solutions promotes balance. Balance, when actively engaged, produces superior results. Here are some evidences:

Balance

1. Is noted for realistic expectations that promote holistic development of the person, enhancing equitable and measured growth and contributions.
2. Develops activities from pure motives so that while excellence is encouraged, a person's overall well-being is kept at the forefront.
3. Encourages creative thinking and action because the person who rests regularly possesses reserves for when action is needed.
4. Reduces stress and the frustrations that usually accompany business, promotes clearer judgment and healthy perspectives because it lives in realism of achievement and properly appreciates success.
5. Focuses energies on causes that count, prioritizing these and prompting better choices for those arenas where energies should be directed.
6. Sees and actively promotes contributions from a selfless and wanting-to-serve position, with strength left over for the next opportunity to provide assistance and support.
7. Contributes to health and healing attitudes and actions within the physical, emotional, mental, and spiritual dimensions, achieving victory as problems are confronted with truth. Balance promotes proportioning strength to meet the challenges of life, refusing artificial substitutes and, while accepting help, determines the will-not-cross lines of behavior, to live within bounds of proper assistance, learning and growing through the experiences.
8. Sharply focuses on proactive solutions, encourages decisions coming from true inspiration and the activities of hard perspiration to accomplish tasks well.
9. Destroys walls that block understanding of relationships and corroborating function, and replaces them with pathways of desired comprehension and encouragement.

10. Generates growth when a team comes together to work on a project, complementing team members through combining efforts, seeking to complete the tasks and the people who fulfill them.
11. Contributes to conclusive communication by molding clarity and character through open and intersecting lines of truth telling.
12. Marks maturing people who actively seek to learn from wiser and more experienced individuals, providing impetus and energy to learn more as they move from one educational goal to the next.
13. Supports those who wish to mature beyond their current development plane, freely encouraging a "no-limit" perspective on greater causes, the dreams and desires that give them life, and the beneficial behavioral changes they embrace.

Certainly balance is preferred over imbalance, if for no other reason than its results are superior. There is, however, a greater cause for achieving balance and it is this: the *process* of incorporating balance into the people of the core team develops great people *as it unfolds*. This process of engagement in healthy practice is actually more important than the product of its efforts, because the process never "ends" until life ceases.

The principles taught and applied, as discipline for balance in work and rest takes hold, promote and sustain health in all four dimensions of the person. Further, within this disciplined process character is honed, nourished and supported. Here the great decisions about life and learning originate, freed from the dead weights of imbalance: those inadvisable and needless expenditures of energy on less worthy goals.

Achieving balance is a worthy aspiration and the great news is this: it is possible to accomplish. Realistic methods to foster its creation and implementation must be learned and applied. No good thing comes about in human-originated experience apart from the desire of the result becoming the motivator of the action. This truth holds true for achieving balance, of course. Its state of well-being will not devolve simply because a person or team agrees that dwelling in its benefits is a good idea. Action makes achieving balance a reality. And the action steps an individual or team produce become their indicators over time of success or failure as behaviors are weighed against effectiveness, then either continued or discarded.

In short, action steps to create balance begin with a sincere desire to gain health, and of necessity *will be calendared*, if true evaluations of efforts are really important. One begins the balance journey with the discipline to incorporate dates and times of balancing activities onto a plan, and in the very act of setting and adhering to the plan, balance starts to come!

The beginning is desire. How hungry are you for balance? When the hunger is great enough, the next move is to action, detailing specifically the moments of rest and work in which you want to engage. Acquiring appropriate and timely permissions, notifying the people on the team — these are essential communication pieces and natural sequential considerations of a workable solution group who seeks to incorporate balance and enjoy its benefits. The tough part is maintaining this truth: that when the calendar is committed, it will be followed, period, no matter what, and that the obligation to that commitment does not falter.

It may sound easy, but if you are a producer and a driven one at that, it is not simple at all. If you work with a team of driven people, it may be harder yet. While intentions are easier to state they are potentially mighty hard to consistently accomplish. Note this truth, please.

Balance is hard to initiate and maintain simply because life's circumstances and work's demands are too often allowed the ruling prioritization. This lack of discipline has severe consequences over time. Conversely, the application of discipline has consequences, too. Where decisions to calendar the specifics of dates, times and events for rest are respected, the people who embark on their balanced journey decisions are honored, and their commitments upheld with a firm and immovable dedication to wholeness from all the members of the core team. Beneficially, the positive results from these good decisions are often seen sooner as opposed to later, and potentially last a lifetime.

The Dates

Our son is age 20 and daughter age 23. When these two precious people were quite young, the son 4 and the daughter 6, a decision was made with us as parents that I would take each family member on a date every month until the kids were married. This commitment and its consistent follow-through have literally changed our lives.

In seminars I am known to express the fact that this idea of the father dating the children and his wife once a month is not original with me and that is true. What may be unique, however, is that I can count on one hand the number of times we have ever missed a monthly date, covering a time frame of 17 years. Recently my daughter reminded me that if we had ever missed, we made it up the next month (two dates in one month!), and as far as I can recall, she is 100% correct in this, which means, of course, that in reality we have never missed one.

At the beginning of every month, on the first or second day of the month, the dates for the family are established for the remainder of the month, the times set aside and, as the date draws closer, the places of rendezvous determined. Anticipation and busy days follow as our schedules intersect and move apart, but no matter what comes, good or bad, that date time is sacred, set apart, upheld, and honored.

Each date with the son or daughter is unique in its way, and each date has its set of conversation topics and places to engage. What are those topics down through the years? Well, usually whatever the kid wants to talk about. And places to go? We have chosen many places to have our dates. When the children were young, a fast-food restaurant and amusement center might fit the bill exactly, and I recall one night on the eve of my son's 13th birthday that all he wanted to do after dinner was go to the beach and throw rocks into the ocean, and that is exactly what we did. Within reasonable expectations, the time, event and place are centered on the kids and their needs, and the amount of the expenses incurred does not determine success or failure. Sometimes spending virtually nothing and taking a long walk and a bike ride are just the things.

When this activity and its merits have been explained to others, often a response sounds like this, "Well, we're together all the time; I take the kids out on occasion." Or, "I really should do this, but I see the kids each night (or day)." And this: "I take them to movies once in a while." Clearly there is nothing wrong with spending occasional and unplanned time, but let me give you the key to the success of the kind of dating relationship with our children that has sown so many good seeds that we have witnessed for many years:

1. It is a duet, only: one child with dad (or parent/guardian) at one time.
2. It is planned in advance: announced, agreed, and calendared.
3. It is regular: the schedule is honored, and it occurs once a month, every month.
4. It is uninterrupted time: the whole thing is dedicated to the child.
5. It is focused: actions, attitudes, topics are chosen and fulfilled with complete attention given to the child. No business, no interruptions. Turn the cell phone off if you must!

As the kids have become adults, the venues have changed, of course, as have the topics of conversation. What have remained are our heart's desires and their unalterable designs to concentrate on the kids and their needs. The dates are precise moments in our month when my full attention is on the perspectives of our children. In fact, when not too long ago my daughter contemplated her future, she asked me if I would date her after she was married. I replied, gently, "No. You will always be my daughter, and you will belong to your husband. But I would be delighted to date you and your husband together if you both agreed to it." On the date that occurred the night before she became engaged to be married, we reaffirmed that desire. The benefits continue, and may outlive us all.

In our model we decided that dad would initiate the dates each month. Of course, families today are composed of many relationships, and some families are without a dad's presence. The parent or guardian of a child, regardless of gender, will find great benefit in considering and deciding to spend dedicated time with the children individually.

But if it is possible for dad to dedicate himself to this discipline, there appears to be an enhanced result that, at least from our experience, is immeasurable. In developing character, influencing choices, taking time, encouraging, celebrating, and wondering together, these activities have affected many of the huge decisions as our lives have progressed, which we now, upon looking back, can measure in terms of best decisions and preferred paths. In the context of seeing results of 17 years of this activity, I state unequivocally that countless life-altering good choices have followed that first great choice to put the family and its importance in high priority and dedicated procedure.

Of course, Mom's opportunity to date the children is important, too. I encourage this whenever it is possible. Her engagement is as vital as is her full agreement that if dad can do this, she wholeheartedly and openly welcomes and supports these adventures with him and the kids. And I will stop here and state unequivocally that the support my wife has given to me for the kid's dating experiences has been nothing short of outstanding, and I am grateful to her beyond words for this.

What matters centrally is the *specific* time and *singularly articulated focus* that *the kid matters*, and that *what matters to each matters to their adult care giver*, and that when together, *the child and parent/guardian will have uninterrupted time to dwell in truth telling, growing, loving, laughing, crying through trial and test, whatever is called for, to help build what is, in itself, a wonderful mix and solution, and an investment the child and the parent or guardian will never forget.*

We have looked at the past many years of child development and we can articulate some of our results here, believing that many of these were born of a decision for dad to invest, and of the dedicated support of mom that he does so:

- We never lost our kids in their teenage years.
- The kids never tried drugs.
- The kids have always wanted to bring their friends to our home and we absolutely love having them there!
- The kids love their parents and know we love them, openly expressing this.
- The kids know for certain that we are absolutely not a perfect family (let's not even go there!).
- The kids also know, however, that we are a family that believes in truth, forgiveness, integrated and honest communication, exercised even when it's difficult or next to impossible to do.
- The kids know we value timely and open confrontation of needful issues and appropriate resolution, as opposed to sweeping agendas under a false covering or artificial mask.
- The kids know we believe in not hiding pain; rather, moving through it to promote learning, loving, living and life.
- The kids are committed to high moral values, attitudes and actions.
- The kids are committed to their faith.

The bottom line: so much of their belief and practice is born of the engagement of creating dedicated and unalterable space and time to grow together, whether with mom or dad. Spending this kind of time has reaped quantitatively positive rewards, and we strongly encourage this kind of engagement for families.

You may be wondering what all of this has to do with balance. The tie-in is this: dedication to right action where attention is pre-focused on rest and play, especially with ones you love, creates a process of discipline, cooperation, and space for growth. In our experience, apart from that discipline, the growth would simply not have occurred to the degree it did. Balance has come in the process and the growth of everyone involved. This process for this author has certainly been an indicator and incubator of longevity of relationships and corroborating functions through-out our formative family years.

While we are still learning the ins and outs of this kind of maturing we are immensely grateful that we have tried it, and we continue to engage in it. For us, balance has been both a process and a continuing product, fostering a continuum of growth we treasure, and for which we would substitute nothing.

Where rest and work in correct alignment are peaceful cohabitants instead of to-the-death competitors, a person's worth is validated and opportunities for growth provided. A commitment to rest and work for any member of a core team is a decision and action born of, and sustained through, full agreement that people are more important than what they do, that relationship (decision) comes before and gives definition to function (task). There may be no greater demonstration of this truth than when people participate freely in the rhythm of life, working and resting, fully supported by superiors and team members, dedicated to the proper equilibrium the actions produce.

It is in that equilibrium that health can be, and often is, realized. A strong and values-based commitment to work comes from a maturing and healthy relationship, and the same kind of commitment to rest is a demonstration of the need to receive strength to re-fill and re-fuel for tomorrow's functions. This kind of balance is part of life's ebb and flow of energy.

Commitments that promote it will sustain and maximize the effectiveness of the person and the team on which he or she serves.

A dedication to work requires discipline to be part of a workable solution; a decision to rest also requires discipline for the good of the worker. Because time away is important enough to schedule, on dedicated teams it will be treated as "sacred," faithfully set apart, regardless of circumstances.

Balance of work and rest is not optional for a growing and effective core team. Proper rest, of course, promotes more function as the cycle is repeated, and the ongoing experiences of both are enjoyed as processes and products unfold, consecutively. As part of its character, rest will always include a preparation for a return to work, but remember this: the preparation to re-enter the fray is only a part of the result desired. The most important and longed-for result from rest is, well, rest.

Driving it home, every core team member should set aside time and time frames in which rest is to occur. And then, those members must absolutely not engage in work during away times, leaving the ties that bind people to their work, at work.

This can be difficult to do because some of these ties, if permitted and not unbound, provide unwanted and "un-needful," "un-deedful" incursions into rest space, away place and timed pace. The "sacredness" of rest is simply not designed to accept unwanted invasions, if it is truly honored.

Incursions can come from many sources. For example, leave the following off or at home: business cell phones, hand-held computers, business satellite phones, business pagers, business tracking devices, business lap tops, business-use global positioning system receivers and varied other methods of contact that, if permitted, could invade your space, place and pace of non-work.

Further, every team member must honor the time apart for any other team member. That honor will be seen in the strength of the team's dedication to keeping the contact channels open, but simply not traversing or transgressing in their paths. In this regard we may have destroyed the idea of the oxymoron called, "the working vacation." An attempted combination of the two depletes the design, focus and energy of each, and probably defeats the intentions of both. This is a mixture from which a core team can and should refrain.

Achieving balance is bringing to pass a state of being where rest and work are apportioned and proportioned definitively, where life's contributions for work are punctuated willfully and willingly with opportunities and engagements for repose and inter-mission breaks. While one person's rest may be another person's racket, the point is that the term that is dedicated for non-work is decided, defined, upheld, supported, celebrated, and evaluated as to its journey (process) and reward (benefit). This journey should be a time of discovery, fresh perspectives brought about through alternate engagements, and its reward at a minimum should be renewed strength for the new opportunities that work and working together provide, as well as the retention of the reserves acquired during the time away.

No excuses here, everyone needs this. It would be beneficial for you and your core team to engage in constructive conversation as to how well you are achieving balance for yourself and the team, right now. If the efforts to pursue and produce balance are not those in which you are engaged presently, and you and the group mutually agree that there are great merits on the journey of achieving balance, this question must be deliberately posed: when will you start to calendar your time of refreshment for yourself, your family, your children, your team, your group, your organization? Of course, this follow up question comes on its heels quickly: when will you implement these important plans, and how will we know?

Chapter 9:
Come, Work Where I Do:
Creating Industrial Strength
Solutions in Your Organization

- "If you could only get this message out to my boss! We really need this!"
- "If you only knew what I put up with around here!"
- "Every business would benefit from these principles."
- "Ok, what if you had a leader like mine that is unapproachable, and wouldn't even take the time of day to consider any of this?"
- "My hands are tied."
- "I'm here, I do my job—I go home."
- "These training programs are all the same. We tried one once and it didn't work. We're not interested in yours."
- "I have no desire to participate in this, at any level. It's a waste of time."
- "Nothing ever changes."
- "I just don't see that starting stuff like this is my responsibility."
- "My boss keeps changing his mind; all I get are mixed signals. That hasn't changed for a long time and probably won't."

- "All we get are empty promises. We hear, 'I'll take care of it' but nothing ever happens."
- "I am very uncomfortable with change, any change."
- "All change has to come from the top."
- "This stuff is not real life."
- "Ah, yes, the next feel-good program!"
- "If only, if only…"
- "I've tried to change stuff here, and I am tired of trying. I only get frustrated if I put forth an effort. It's not worth it."
- "I am only important because of what I do."
- "We are so messed up here, nothing would work."
- "My work is the last place that would ever consider this."
- "I hate it here, I hate coming to work."
- "No one listens to me, so why bother?"
- "I am getting my resume together. Anything's better than this rat hole."
- "They pay me way too much money to upset (name of employer)."
- "This is confidential, right? If they ever heard I was talking about this, my job would be toast."
- "Affirmation? Yea, right…"
- "There is too much at stake. I'd face recrimination if I took these ideas to the people that really need to hear them."
- "I'd lose my job, or (co-worker or boss's name) could make my life miserable around here."
- "There is no way!"

You would be correct if you concluded that these are actual quotes from people in organizations who recognize and, in some cases, wallow in ongoing and pervasive dysfunction. These comments come from people who see palpable needs for vital change, for an infusion of health, for a working industrial strength solution environment, even though they don't use those words. The expressions of dissatisfaction and disallowance of engagement are not limited to the list above, of course; many of the quotes are those with language I deem as not appropriate to print.

For their own reasons, the people who live and work in environments like those described above are disagreeable, immobile, cowering or running away from responsibility, either through their own choices, or brought about from feelings that convince them that telling truth, going "out on the limb," offering right words and showcasing better actions to promote health won't produce any changes anyway. Or, they truly fear confrontation, convincing themselves that they would lose. They are willfully allowing just plain fear of negative fallout, recrimination, or embarrassment to stand in the way of shouldering accountability and initiative, choosing instead to dwell in victimization and excuses and, as was shown in Chapter 6, trying in some cases to align with a power center to avoid responsibility. This does not represent a pleasant environment in which to work, and clearly is not part of an industrial strength solution.

Perspectives become tried and true in challenging business environments, and no two are, or ever will be, the same. Work atmospheres and cultures vary from enterprise to enterprise and the complex nature of business and exacting demands of customer and vendor provision foster ever-changing environments where good choices and solid characters are placed and tested. Application of principles into real life has always been where the common rubber and roads connect. Once again, an individual or core team who truly desires growth, and who wants to contribute within workable solutions, is forced to consider this: if a system of learning and living is proven through time to build better results for those involved then am I, are we, *willing* to take what we *know* is truth and make it *live* in our own daily experiences, even if it means *fundamental change*?

Inhibitors (people) and inhibitions (circumstances) confront the person who seeks to know and grow, but these should and must not be allowed to be the end game. The negatives can become opportunities for investments within industrial strength solutions if they are treated as part of the overall journey of living and learning, and are conquered with the truth that good principles work, every time they are tried.

There is no pre-qualification that says that healthy change must proceed from the top down in an organization. This perception merely agrees with the perceived but incorrect notion that if a positive change is to occur, its only chance for success is that it is initiated from the top. Experience proves otherwise. Excuses for inaction should be replaced with causes for purposed activity, regardless of position, where belief is sure that the cause is more important than the dysfunction. Of course, mutual agreements for functional, provisional, process-oriented and procedural changes should be obtained from the right people in the right ways. But if we are talking character, competence and caring, and the workable solutions of The Four Decisions and The Four Standards, then no prior approval is needed if a core team or any of its membership yearn to excel from an earnest desire to become part of something better. Here are the decisions and standards again, for review:

The Four Decisions:
Turning Whining into Winning

Turn habits of complaining into habitats of constructing.	**Replace** negative attitudes with positive solution-focused outlooks.	**Redirect** an ego-centered focus to concentrating on benefiting others.	**Confront** problems with positive planning and action steps.

The Four Standards:
The Constitution of Workable Solutions

Integrity The quest and expression of truth	**Decision-Making** The choices you make that count	**Commitment** The point where decisions become actions	**Faithfulness** The proof of when duty is fulfilled well

Purposed change is founded squarely on what is known to be preferable, proven through time and test. Therefore, purposed change begs to be given the chance to be born and develop *especially in relationships*, which are the decisions a core team member makes about another's success, the action verbs and powerful intangibles listed in the tables above.

Certainly it is right and needful for a person to know his or her place and status within an organization and, where one has earned a right to be listened to, that person can promote causes that within character and practice have already been proven reliable through personal modeling. The responsibility for the person who believes change is needful rests with him or her. That individual becomes the one who takes the initiative to live it first and promote it second. This pattern lives through their experiences and the positive demonstrations of excellence they manifest, where truth is produced in real life.

Once an individual has committed to a plan of action based on desired need, the process of the action becomes more important than the product, and will dictate long-term strength of applied principle if accomplished well. Getting started, though, can be tough, especially when the person with the idea has not yet achieved the station that commands attention and respect or the honor that comes from someone else listening with a true interest, because a model has not yet been observed.

A process of healthy change should be generated from a committed individual into a close group of associates within the nearest network, often peers. And here exists an added challenge: peers are the ones who probably know the idea-person best and, because of that knowledge, already have an intimate understanding of the truthfulness and reliability of the ideas and actions of this individual. They have either seen these maxims integrated and interrelated positively, producing success, or they have witnessed a whole lot of change ideas without needful and supporting action. If complaints without solutions have been heard, they may constitute nothing more than whining, and whining is not a mark of credibility. We've already covered that unfortunate state and its fruitlessness.

An individual who wants to change the circumstances of a

work group, create an industrial strength solution in his or her workplace, has to start with answering these fundamental questions:

1. How much am I willing to change, first?
2. How willing am I to earn the credibility that will impact and influence others by creating the change in me that they can see, consistently?

In other words, for change notions to become change motions, the actions coming from new ideas must conform to actions from the idea generator, first. The bottom line is this: it starts with you, if you are the one who desires positive change. If it doesn't start with you, then the projection is that the truth would work elsewhere but not here, and isn't that too bad that we have to work and live like this when change of the current situation would be so much better, if only, if only…(whine, whine, whine…)?

> The responsibility for the person who believes change is needful rests with him or her. That individual becomes the one who takes the initiative to live it first and promote it second.

Change of relationship-driven action doesn't have to originate from the top. While there are perceived and real benefits if it is generated there, positive alteration really comes from the committed, regardless of station. Those who articulate and activate truth in their own lives demonstrate that an idea for healthy change is worthy of an audience above, across from, or below.

Is an idea generator willing to become fully enmeshed in the intertwining responsibilities that come with the dedication of this decision: "I will change me first, and show you that it works…" before disingenuously requiring that change comes from the top? Has the idea generator ever shown the top the true benefits of the ideal changes desired and proposed? Has the top even been given the benefit of solution provision coming from underneath where clear initiative has been taken, actions followed through, and positive results provided, first?

Change begins with its originator. If the idea person desires change enough to be willing to incorporate and prove it into his or her life, then possibly a precursor to requiring that others consider change, too, can be born. Nothing speaks louder or longer in a quest for credibility than an in-advance application of principle, proven true through time and in multiple circumstances.

Let's conclude that a core team has generated and proposed needful change in their desires to constitute a workable solution, that the ideas, initiation, and implementation of one or two forward-thinking and reliable people created their hunger for something better in terms of working relationships. Let's observe that their principle-based processes have created and are developing a duplicating model that can and should be tried in other modes and work cultures. Let's verify that through their consistent actions they are proving that no matter where principles are confirmed and deeds conform to truth, the applications bear witness: principled truth does not flex or bend with circumstances. Were we to see a team thus engaged, we could conclude:

1. This team is demonstrating that desired change rests on foundations that don't.
2. This team is proving that the result is transformation for the better.
3. This team commands attention!

Know upon what your foundations of principle rest. Know your environment and know yourself, and why you believe what you believe. Plan and place your desires, learning and application into your situation. Engage in the process of relational development fully, treasure and celebrate the results, and then look for ways of broader dissemination. Others will notice because they have to, whether or not the credit for the successes returns to the original idea person. Change first because *you* need to. Then seek to spur change in others that may be deemed needful.

If you are the one who seeks to see change occur for the better, appreciate that this process begins and is given momentum through desires that you turn into deeds. Deeds matched to needs, in cooperation with principles, produce powerful displays of passion that energize processes toward beneficial outcomes. Become part of that wholesome pattern and watch advantageous change start to happen!

A Strategic Plan

Consider designing a strategic plan to accomplish the positive changes you deem needful. Strategy, as defined in *Industrial Strength Solutions*, is a carefully designed plan encompassing purpose and methodology to accomplish a desired goal. Your strategy will include specific tactics, defined as specific systems, applications and modes. Strategy and tactics cooperate to fulfill the ultimate and beneficial desires (opportunities for success).

A strategic plan will include factors of time, roles and responsibilities, degrees of risk, thorough knowledge of inhibitors, evaluation of process, re-appraisals and corrections and adjustments of applications as progress is made or new challenges are uncovered. Methods of engagement will include appraisal and appropriation of personnel and materiel resources, acquisition of new assets, operational time lines, and ongoing reappraisals of conditions and environments.

To affect good changes in your organizational environment, apply your strategy and tactics to your activities and contributions, first. Then, tried and tested, these proven results from your plan can be widened to include your network and a broader audience of participants and observers.

Your specific methods will include establishing action, setting a start date, implementation, integration with other resources and teams, networking of shared results, and full reporting of success or failure. Further, because you agree with your core team and company value system, steps involved in your strategic plan and methods will not violate values or sacrifice integrity. Truth will stand and, when it is employed fully from the person who takes the initiative and then is accountable to quality fulfillment of the plan and the purpose behind the plan, change results are noteworthy and contributory, building up, not tearing down, a true win.

Your strategic plan and its methods can become a vehicle for you to design mixtures of resources and measurements of results, the repeatable formulas that assure that the changes you desire in your work environment, when accomplished in right ways and for the right reasons, will provide concrete and tested prescriptions that can be replicated in other work environments. Where people long for uplifting changes, repeatable models are the ones upon which longevity is built; where they are seen to work in one place, they will work in another.

The one who first sees the need can become the instigator of the change that compels others to sit up and take notice, and perhaps become engaged, because the success of a principle is transferable and desirable. The proof is this: it has been seen to work within you.

Designing a strategic plan and specific tactics of preferred change institution includes these action steps:

1. Define the needs, the areas where, if positive change is created, perceived and real good results will benefit participants and their networks, as well as observers.
2. Envision the results of solutions, the kind of environments or provisions that, if accomplished, will produce better results.
3. Align your dream with specific desires for change.
4. Decide the degree of your effort needed for change to

occur. Is it worth your energy? If so, proceed; if not, refrain from living in the quagmire of the problem and certainly no more whining about it. Forget it and move on.

5. Commit to needed change within you, first, to help meet the need.
6. List and fulfill the behavioral changes to which you will be dedicated.
7. Change your behavior, observe and celebrate your results.
8. When your results have been proven, then incorporate others who share your desires, to engage with you toward positive alterations.
9. Share the success stories within your team's environment.
10. Design a strategic plan with your group and obtain necessary permission to institute broader change.
11. Prepare your group to confront obstacles with grace, forthright and respectful conversation, holding fast to principle and agreed values.
12. Re-design any elements of your plan shown to need readjustment.
13. Set a timeline for implementation of the approved plan.
14. Engage the group in doing the deeds that meet and fulfill the needs.
15. Evaluate, correct, and celebrate.
16. Display the model, its motives and methods, to other groups who desire healthy change.
17. Be prepared to explain the process and its product, giving more emphasis to the process. Remember, within the process phase is where true growth occurs in you, and others with you.
18. Become a student and active participant of the procedure of change and the wholeness of the solution process; then, do it over again.

Action steps must be created and fulfilled, otherwise the dream and desires for alterations in your work mix will remain only concepts. The key here is that action in realistic time lines is followed through. Actions within a plan for change are not optional, if the plan is to succeed. When obstacles present themselves, bent on preventing forward movement, move on this: resolve is strengthened through renewed initiative, positive motive, greater communication, more proofs, continual caring about people and open confrontation of issues. Don't be side tracked. Truth outweighs, outshines and outlives trouble.

The Balancing Action

John is a successful businessman, achieving favorable outcomes over many productive years in the construction industry in a fast-developing sector of the country. In reading and assimilating the factors of industrial strength solutions, John has become a student of principle, seen in renewed commitments to truth-telling and focused follow-through. While continuing to fulfill complicated and integrated multi-tiered tasks for another of the area's premier building and contracting firms, he endeavors to balance his active work schedule with his home and family life.

In the course of his journeys of being a leader and a follower, John has many times faced dilemmas that can only be addressed with blatant truth in atmospheres of growing understanding and, at times, pointed conflict resolution. To quote John, "Timing of the job and the need for consistent communication is forcing a realignment of how I communicate. Truth-telling must remain my primary focus, regardless of what I am going through. The question is this: how do we tell the truth, plan for the future—promote and live in the truth at the same time?" It's a great question. For John, as for all those who have to project outcomes in a realistic framework while planning for and achieving the biggest wins and the most desired financial rewards, it is sometimes easier to promise more than can be delivered, and to try to make up differences through methods whose tenets can violate values, if taken to the extreme.

Achieving efficiency in balance with good character means an ongoing and dedicated reallocation of resources to meet goals, while showcasing integrity throughout the process. Clarification of a plan is necessary to agreement on what the goals are, and implementation of any plan should be time sensitive while never sacrificing proper and ethical procedures.

Part of the intense struggle occurs when people get taken for granted in the movement and management of properties and buildings. One of John's tough considerations when he was interviewed was this: when it's hard for an employer to recognize inherent and earned values of an employee, what should the responsibility be, if any, for a manager who wants to tell the employer to wake up and tangibly reward good quality? This is no small item and, after considerable deliberation, the following conclusions made a lot of sense:

- We will not impugn motive; we can only observe activity.
- The manager (or influencer) should recognize the situation for what it is, taking a neutral stance.
- The manager should obtain explicit permission to address conditions with the people involved, presenting truthful facts, and proposing solutions designed to build a win-win for all parties.
- The manager will showcase proven change in his or her operations, first.
- The manager will help create and implement a solution plan.
- The plan will include measurable evaluations in a specified time frame that allow for growth and reward.
- The process will protect integrity and will not play one end against the middle, and the influencer assures this.
- The manager will tell the truth, combining commensurate value with legitimate reward, to initiate and sustain a mutually agreeable system in which all parties agree to participate.

Integrity, truth-telling, faithfulness, affirmation and examination of expected outcomes are integrated, and become measurements of the desire to "do it right" for everyone who acts as a catalyst for change. John is acquainted with "Cooperative Problem Solving and Conflict Resolution," a technique explained and charted in *Leadership Is—*, pages 74-79, and 120. This resolution process combines values agreement and appropriate action and, as John has employed the technique, he has experienced the wider and positive impact the technique seeks to produce.

I asked John toward the end of our interview for *Industrial Strength Solutions* what changes he still wants to make that he knows are solution-oriented and will promote good character. His reply was revealing: "Obtaining buy-in for necessary change occurs through understanding of how a broader goal, or collection of them, benefits both employer and employees at the same time. Buy-in builds strength within the company and stronger provision to customers, constructing a future and a hope of implementation for everyone involved." Now that is value-added, a decision firmly rooted in the welfare of all, soundly based on shared agreement of what is truly important.

If positive change is desired it must be first acquired within the one who wants it the most. Fulfilled through a growing model of faithful adherence to core values, its credibility may then be shared with those who are becoming convinced, because they have witnessed true success. It is then that building a productive work environment is possible. Let's move forward and get it done.

Chapter 10: Building a Productive Work Environment

When desire, based on dedicated doctrine, outweighs difficult and disturbing distractions, its decisive action declares that truth, in real life, works. If the environment in which you work needs to be altered, you may be the one who takes the necessary risks to make it happen, who causes others to listen and learn from you because you have so lived the principles in practice that your experience has produced positive outcomes others want.

The one who takes the initiative becomes the point person of proof. Don't ask others to change unless you are willing to change initially to demonstrate the validity of the action. With this kind of responsibility at stake it stands to reason that many will shirk and shrink from the option of taking initial hits. But for those who pursue, profitable and quantifiable working solutions will have far better opportunities for success.

It begins, of course, with your desire. What do you want, why do you want it, and how willing are you to pay the costs in order to get it? Far from a philosophy that if you "exclaim it and claim it," it will "surely happen," and "it will feel really good, too," this stuff frankly is very hard work, feelings are not the focus, and there are many who propose but do not close. Many ideas, a lot of talk, but no positive actions equal chronic disappointment and lack of credibility, and a growing void of confidence that the person with the ideas can be counted on at all.

Promises made and not kept, commitments positioned in the emotion of the moment without true desires and means to accomplish those ends, produce vagueness and vacuums that are filled with cheap substitutes and a lot of excuses. If you want change, you will change. You will initiate and follow through. It's that simple. And it all begins with your desire.

"Catalyst" is a term that describes one who brings positions and people together. According to *Merriam-Webster's 11th Collegiate Dictionary*, a catalyst is also "a substance that enables a chemical reaction to proceed at a usually faster rate or under different conditions." Such is the case in creating industrial strength solutions that work. The person who truly desires a core team to increase its strength of relationships and output of functional excellence will become the catalyst of provision that he or she is meant to be, if those beneficial alterations are to become reality. That person's motives for positive change are integrity and initiative. These motives help that person see the rewards expected over time. One motivated with these does not give in, and positively will not give up.

> When desire, based on dedicated doctrine, outweighs difficult and disturbing distractions, its decisive action declares that truth, in real life, works.

The Contest

Many years ago I was engaged in competitive speech and, through the processes associated with these endeavors, began to learn (and, by the way, I am still learning) the benefits of determination, especially when a cause was worth the efforts needed for completion. A service club organization provided an initial teaching experience when it offered to freshmen and sophomore high school young men the opportunity of competing in an international speech tournament, for which the prize of winning first place out of 40,000 competitors, was a college scholarship. The speech tournament rules required that to move from one level to the next, a first place must be obtained at every level. So I began the journey and achieved success at the local, regional, and district levels. Then the going got tougher.

The semi-final round consisted of 40 competitors, 5 groups of 8 each, all 15 or 16 years of age, who had achieved a degree of notoriety just by arriving at this level, who earnestly desired to get in "the final round" where, of course, the winner would take all. The semi-final rounds were scheduled, and the results were eagerly anticipated back at home. I was encouraged, hopeful, and wanting to win the big prize. Before the semi-finals commenced, the "host" or "home town" club had set up a special phone line for me to communicate with the club when the semi-final victory was won. The phone was red, which added some perceived importance to the nature of its use, especially in that "cold war" era. My phone call as a finalist was awaited by club members assembled on the other end of the line, anxious to hear that victory was in reach, with only the final round to go.

But my presentation in the semi-final round was not one of my best performances; in fact, it fell far short of the mark of excellence that in other rounds had won the current levels achieved. Bottom line, I bombed.

It was a grim experience to gather with a representative of the club who had traveled to the competition with me and explain to the assembled club membership over that red phone that their prize contender had not made it into the final round. It was an awkward conversation at the outset to be sure. But there was one aspect that I considered as the phone call progressed, which I decided to communicate before it concluded. You see, at the time of this contest I was 15 and, according to the rules of the contest, I had one additional year to go should I choose to re-enter; the top age for any contestant for this service club speech tournament was 16. If I wanted to, I could try once more. I decided that I most assuredly wanted this. Through that red phone I told the folks listening on the other end that I would try again. Cheers resounded but victory would have to wait. It would be a long road: as with every contestant, I would have to start at the very beginning when the opportunity came around the next year.

Time passed and, as the next year's speech tournament opportunity dawned, I wrote a speech, memorized it, practiced delivery technique, and entered the contest. I approached the local level competition with confidence and a strong desire to make good on the "I will try again" promise. Winning at the first level created the opportunity of competing at a subsequent level, and fortunately, the process of winning continued until I found myself at the semi-final round level, again. This time the stakes seemed to be higher as the club celebrated its 50th Anniversary, and while there was no red phone, the real consequences were the same, nonetheless. The scholarship prize emerged as perhaps within my grasp once more.

Again, 40 contestants entered the semi-finals, 5 groups of 8, out of a pool of 40,000 or so that had entered at the local levels weeks before. Now out of these semi-final contestants emerged 5 finalists, and amazingly, I was one of them. The sheer consequence of deciding to re-enter that competition, of trying again and getting this far, made me shake my head in unbelief that I had done it, but then, quickly, a new and stark realization emblazed its impression on my psyche: there was a lot of work still left to do here! The final push had become the most important one, so I set my mind and energies to get to it.

The final round occurred on the day following the semi-finals. Speaking to an assemblage of 3,000 people in the local sports arena for the concluding speech contest event remains a treasured memory and, even in those pre-cassette and pre-CD days, a recording, a small 45 record, was made of the presentation. Convincing myself that this was the moment and opportunity for which 24 months of preparation and desire had prepared me, I delivered my oration, the crowd applauded (as they did each contestant), and upon finishing the oration, I took my seat with four other young men to await the judges' decision.

There were many lessons enfolded into the series of events that had led to this moment. The final outcome of this particular speech tournament contributes little to the most important aspects and truths to be embraced, so it will go untold here. But one of the most important lessons was this: *the desire and dedication applied early on to pursue a path of hard and even harder work, because the process and its product were deemed needful and advantageous, was a worthwhile pay-off, regardless of the result.*

In this former day, many years ago, when efforts at achievement were rewarded in a world of high school competition with scholarship funds to advance higher learning, many experiences helped shape one young man for entering another contemporary world where the rewards are often harder to come by, events more disconcerting, efforts far more complicated and work place environments not as contributory to encouragement like that offered on the other end of the red phone.

In the real work world, values are challenged as to their validity when the environments that surround them provide atmospheres that promote winning at any price. Right reasons and motives, regardless of who the "competition" is are not always displayed or preferred. Competition can get ugly in contemporary commerce where winning is only defined as another person, team or company's defeat. In part, of course, it is true that competition in a free marketplace sets these lines of demarcation.

But competition in another form is that which seeks internal improvement, competing with one's self to make that person the best he or she can be. This kind of competition promotes healthy individuals who, with others of like mind and motive, join in a freedom of production where encouragement and agreed values win the day. Here, competition and personal responsibility combine to set up best models of relationship and function that become the impetus for helping others who want to improve.

Both aspects of competition are with us, and the former usually is highlighted over the latter. But when paradigms of competing against others are replaced with patterns of competing against ourselves, so that the individual strives to become the best he or she can become, that process empowers others to benefit from the encouragements such activities promote, and more enduring core team health is the result.

Abraham Lincoln, in discussing the responsibilities of a lawyer, said this: "Discourage litigation. Persuade your neighbors to compromise whenever you can. As a peacemaker the lawyer has superior opportunity of being a good man. There will still be business enough." Imagine words like that from a lawyer to other lawyers! But what applies to lawyers who wish to be good men will apply to anyone who, in business, seeks the path of hard work and responsibility for the benefit of others. There will be business enough.

> The one who takes the initiative becomes the point person of proof.

The person who desires change, who promotes and proves it first in his or her actions, becomes the model who perseveres because the cause is right and the benefits many, a sure "connector" of good ideas and best actions, a "catalyst" to bring people and causes together for maximum best deliverables. Where the goal is large enough, the reasons sure enough and the foundational principles enduring enough, there exists abundant motivation and reserves to accomplish a sought-after result, if the desire is strong enough. The person of proof has the most influence on those who observe and interact because the melding of motives is seen to produce the evidences most courageously pursued. The individual who provides the most workable solutions is always one who has been through the test and not only survived, but thrived, because enduring principles will always pave the way of the right and true. Become the connector and the catalyst through your desire, dedication and devotion to duty so that others will see, appreciate and emulate your success.

Healthy change takes time, sometimes more time than an originator plans or anticipates. But time is a necessary ingredient and may be deemed either a blessing or a curse, depending on how it is utilized, managed, and maintained. When the status quo has existed for a long time, a time line for change may be hard to establish. But if the motive is right, the person who desires healthy change has to be creative as change is sought and processes wrought for the good of the whole.

The most important truth-in-life lesson here is that the *process* of creating a workable solution that contributes to industrial strength will be more important than the product, and will use time as an ally, not an opponent. Confidence in outcome becomes sure in the knowledge that "right makes might," to quote Lincoln again, this time from his 1860 speech at Cooper Union. Unwavering assurance in best outcomes gives cause for endurance when challenges increase. People who want best outcomes will see change productivity as a result of best practices, they themselves becoming authors and finishers, the initiators of not only ideas for change, but of the implementations in their own lives and experiences to see the changes through.

Results and rewards come to the one who sees change as needful and willfully and willingly alters his or her person, first. The benefits of healthy change validate the generator; they also generate improvements in the conditions of others in exponential degrees, surpassing even anticipated returns. Leaders who build legacy know this, and this process is described in depth in *Leadership Is—*. Followers and core team members come to realize this truth, too: that when sought-after changes work first in themselves, they cause waves of better attitudes, aptitudes and actions from others. Needful and favorable changes that honor principle and promote industrial strength solutions will integrate into many layers of an organization or work group over time, and become contagious if prompted and promoted from right motives and used in right ways.

You, if you are a core team member who wants to be part of an industrial strength solution, can become the person who makes the decision whether or not to begin, regardless of your title, position, experience or expertise. To help you consider this decision, you may wish to ask yourself these important questions, the answers to which can help you know if you are ready for this mix of principle and practice:

1. If you see a need for change, how willing are you to fulfill it by changing your behavior first?
2. How much cost for a greater cause that will improve other's lives are you willing to consider and pay?
3. How will you face setbacks?
4. How willing are you to tell others of your desires to grow, openly declaring intent and accountability?
5. When circumstances or people around you encourage the negative, how much will their adverse influences cause you to shift or change your good focus to align yourself with something other than the cause in which you first believed?
6. Do you see yourself as a catalyst and contributor in bringing other people together to accomplish something great and, if so, when will you start to engage in behavior that causes other people to want to become involved?
7. How willing are you to achieve change success and not receive the credit?
8. How important is your title or position in initiating the changes you want?
9. How does your utilization of time position you for success or failure?

10. If you could start over, and change sooner, what would you do differently?
11. When will you start over?
12. What stands in the way of needful change beginning within yourself now?
13. What contributes to your not believing in yourself, if this is your current condition?
14. What influences or impacts in your life should you discard that presently serve to discourage or demoralize you?
15. What attributes of helping others succeed can you employ to motivate you toward instituting healthy change?
16. If you changed, who would notice?
17. If you don't change, what or who will?
18. If your character is swayed by circumstance, who can alter this?
19. Upon what value system do you base your desires to institute needful change?
20. When will you initiate deeds to fulfill worthwhile needs?
21. How important do you consider yourself to be in an environment where change is clearly needed?

Those who rise from lesser to greater character may not be people on whom accolades are poured. Yet, those whose conquests consist of taming their inmost struggles are the truest of persons revered, restored.

Self-controlled dedication to right intent for right reasons will outlast severest trials especially when one's character, though his or her name may not be known, shines through the contributions that live beyond the imperfections of now. Such constitutes the character and activity of the catalyst for change, the person who begins with desire, and stays deliberately focused on the higher goal.

If

If you can keep your head when all about you
Are losing theirs and blaming it on you;
If you can trust yourself when all men doubt you,
But make allowance for their doubting too;
If you can wait and not be tired by waiting,
Or, being lied about, don't deal in lies,
Or, being hated, don't give way to hating,
And yet don't look too good, nor talk too wise;

If you can dream—and not make dreams your master;
If you can think—and not make thoughts your aim;
If you can meet with triumph and disaster
And treat those two imposters just the same;
If you can bear to hear the truth you've spoken
Twisted by knaves to make a trap for fools,
Or watch the things you gave your life to broken,
And stoop and build 'em up with wornout tools;

If you can make one heap of all your winnings
And risk it on one turn of pitch-and-toss,
And lose, and start again at your beginnings
And never breathe a word about your loss;
If you can force your heart and nerve and sinew
To serve your turn long after they are gone,
And so hold on when there is nothing in you
Except the Will which says to them: "Hold on";

If you can talk with crowds and keep your virtue,
Or walk with kings—nor lose the common touch;
If neither foes nor loving friends can hurt you;
If all men count with you, but none too much;
If you can fill the unforgiving minute
With sixty seconds' worth of distance run—
Yours is the Earth and everything that's in it,
And—which is more—you'll be a Man my son!

—Rudyard Kipling (1889)

It comes down to innermost and earnest desire, yours, that is based on character, integrity and a value system birthed in right and enduring principle. Your job is to create and undertake a change of heart and attitude receptivity within yourself, not expect it from someone else. When you change yourself, then you are in the best position to consider instituting change within your group.

Think long and hard on this, and if you agree, act. Decide to get it done, create your strategic plan, cultivate tactics to support the overall plan in a desired time line, and start your implementation. Evaluate, correct, and realign as you go. Celebrate your wins and learn from your losses. Engage in effective time management so as to utilize that resource as your needful ally, and be assured of success based on principles that endure.

Industrial strength solutions are modeled through people who see a need and seek to fulfill it. These people understand that solutions don't just evolve; they devolve from purposed individuals who become involved proactively in originating right mixes of people and production, work and rest, in a balanced formula that promotes people first, and product next. These people are the heart of a team that desires best practices from dedication to core values and the value systems they represent.

Far from just thinking their dreams may become reality, their heart's desires cause them to envision outcomes and engage in character-aligned processes. In these they are confident that over time right processes will bear products worthy of their operations. They know that the process is more important than the product because where the process lives, it changes lives, and the advantageous products naturally follow. This kind of thinking is bold, and this action courageous, because this way of interaction often goes against the tide of popular sentiment that is cemented in its status quo, and jack hammers its way into new forms, formulas and formations that endure because they are designed and constructed better.

Expended efforts for higher-cause change exceed wasted energy, and winning attitudes replace whining voices. The worth of the heightened cause is motivated by the worthwhile character traits of the people who make it happen. These are the ones who create endurance-living answers that solve the discomfitures of a workplace culture suffering from its own inadequacies. These people set the model of improvement first in the attitudes and operational actions of the person who desires the change. Desires for expanded competencies and growth in knowledge and productivity come from correct and informed choices about options and opportunities. The dedication to fulfill the goal, "whatever it takes" when the cause is right, creates the impetus to follow through, regardless of cost.

Improved attitudes, aptitudes and actions are necessary to foster innovative and effective solution mixes of people and productivity. People who want to be part of great change choose these attributes eagerly. They see their work environment as a laboratory for developing industrial strength solutions, combining these essential ingredients: holistic view, wholeness, humility and firm resolve, so that, when mixed properly, they produce strength and stability.

You are invited to consider this question: are you the instigator for change in this fashion?

After

At a meeting of leaders and team members with whom Creative Team Resources Group, Inc., www.ctrg.com, was working, the facilitator made it plain from the outset that, as a result of this meeting and subsequent ones, behavioral change should and would be expected, that discussions about what needed to improve in leadership or team activity across the board would only come to open fruition when behavioral change was initiated "at home," beginning in the heart of each leader or participant, preceding others, providing a model for the rest of their teams and participants to emulate. This perspective was a challenge to these collected colleagues and framed that meeting and subsequent ones on the immovable basis of required expectations of results, not mere deliberations of status and consideration of options for improvement alone.

While this particular group realized that knowing about a problem, its source, and its current effects was a necessary consideration of turning negative situations around, they resolved that creating an industrial strength solution mandated a mixing, sifting, and deliberate receiving of solid information, followed by a series of dedicated actions to transform great ideas into realistic and provable operations. In these operations, tenacity to truth was to be permanently affixed to every action, from the smallest assignment to the most imposing project. This prospect moved this group mightily as it may move the team on which you serve.

Entering discussions on the merits of planning and execution where calendaring of actions is required before people leave the room, may cause those who have no desire to participate in more than whining to depart, so that the winners are free of encumbrances to their winning actions. Comments composed of "We need to…" and "Yeah, but…" in a productive environment are obliterated by the initiative takers who seek to own solutions and present them ahead of due dates, with excellence.

So, what should a core team do with its whiners? As hard as it may be to state, but with as much compassion as is possible, to those who desire little beyond mediocrity—"There's the door." While winners won't harbor malice, they will not be impeded by slothfulness, negativity, laziness and unreliability, either. Winners will tolerate little or no continuance of blame, negative "we can't do that" attitudes, complaining comments, lack of initiative and follow-through, and an absence of faithfulness on a core team otherwise consisting of people that truly want to contribute out of strength, who are willing and eager to work together constructively to accomplish their goals, and build their people, at the same time.

Core teams that comprise workable solutions invade negatives with perspectives born of what can be, not what isn't. While they respect the walls of concern, conflict, untried ideas, and uncharted territories, they face them with courage, consistency, principle, and pro-action, believing convincingly that possibilities outweigh and out-perform predispositions of failure. Not content for a moment in dwelling in the reasons why not, and the wastelands of the tired "I don't knows," great core teams look for, create, formulate and inculcate opportunities of engagement into experiences of discovery through sheer grit, founded on sure ground of values-driven desires for growth and excellence. Their proving grounds are their work ethics born of a solid work ethic. These teams produce enduring results that are noticed because they are accomplished well.

Perhaps you will say, "I would be one of those people. I would serve on a team of like-minded and values-focused individuals. I would gather around me others of like passion and, with proper permission, garner the respect of others who view us through the changes we accomplish, and want to engage with us because they see the truths of principle and practice alive within us."

A Core Team is a vehicle of industrial strength solutions, a functional unit that exists on a balance of relationship (decisions about each other's successes) and function (task completion with excellence and high accountability, proving the integrity of the relationship). Its configuration may alter over time but its inherent constitution does not. Regardless of whom it is made, its principles will never change as long as the people who share its premises know that with time and diligence they will participate in its promise. The promise is not perfection; rather, it is fulfillment coming from perseverance of a worthwhile goal, achieving great product through great people who work together well because they earnestly desire to engage in this way.

Desire forms dedicated actions and, ultimately, destiny. The distinguishing marks of good desires are found in the basic character and solid agreements of the individuals that constitute the core team. Ultimately, desire comes to life in behavioral changes where habits of complaining are turned into constructive contributions, where negative attitudes are replaced with positive outlooks, egocentric perspectives are redirected toward views of helping others, and problems are confronted with positive and confident action, replacing misery and whining.

People who come together with those behavioral change-goals in mind are best positioned to exercise constructive decision making. Through their combined commitments they institute industrial strength solutions and the by-products that come from them: better teams of people producing superior products.

The core team has no misty illusions about a "feel good" program that evaporates when difficult problems accumulate. The core team knows that challenges are part of the daily business grind for nearly everyone. The team's members expect that application of principle is hard work, and embrace it. They know their characters are on display whenever they come to produce, and they persevere for unaltered, tenacious and supportive connections between relationship and function, people and production.

Core team participants are mindful that their smaller victories contribute to, and often define, larger wins. They know that the returns for personal and combined competence are increased opportunities, tangible and intangible rewards, and they seek them all. They understand that intangibles prepare the way for tangibles, so with overt and contagious enthusiasm they celebrate their achievements and anticipate the next opportunities for greater accomplishments.

The mix of people on an *Industrial Strength Solutions* core team encourages right positional perspectives as an engagement is planned, understanding their goals and setting up realistic expectations. They play to each other's strengths as they engage in healthy personnel placements. They welcome performance evaluation procedures like those used in the Personnel Review and Planning Document (PRPD) and the Position Account and Contribution Evaluation (PACE) form, both of which include views and evaluations of the twin contributions of relational and functional behaviors. They are anxious to become better, produce more, give their organization heightened output, and generate great deliverables in principle and practice.

A holistic view of the greater cause helps break up the action into doable pieces. This is an evidence of a team's wholeness, where agreed values form the basis of action and reaction, in balance. Core team members make up working solutions and individually choose preferring another person or persons above him or her self. They do this because they are convinced that true humility paves the path of great contributions from humanity, where no one cares who gets the credit and no one dwells in blame.

Living and contributing in wholeness does not assure that good feelings will be the just rewards; in fact, engagement in this perspective is incredibly hard to activate and acclimate, because it objectively views and aligns what may feel good currently with what may be decidedly detrimental in the long run so proper corrections can be made. A true workable solution requires and demands firm resolve and unwavering commitment where success aligns with agreed values and where motives and methods exemplify dedication to consistency, regardless of how the process may feel.

A reigning factor of right people in right practice is the dedication to achieving balance, shown in understanding, agreement, and application of calendared times for work and rest. People on a core team who desire balance for themselves and the organization in which they contribute will not be content with hoping it happens; they will make it happen.

It all begins with desire. If you want to create and be part of an industrial strength solution, act. Use your strength of character to decide to change yourself, first. Others will notice, some will support, many will admire, and a few will join. Work with them.

You will make an incredible difference, whether you know it or not. You may live long enough to view great and lasting contributions that came about because you were willing to become fully engaged in activities based on desire and principle. When will you begin?

Creative
Team
Resources
Group

Resource Needs Assessment (RNA)

<u>Process Description</u>:

We recognize we have resources that need to be thoroughly identified, and allocated appropriately to the accomplishment of tasks. To fully determine what our resources are, we will employ a tool called the Resource Needs Assessment (RNA). In this process our goals will be to clearly identify current resources, understand how they are allocated, create ways we can improve our allocation, and discover projected resources acquisition needs, to help us serve our existing operations better and prepare us for future growth.

There are three primary categories of resources:

1. <u>Personnel</u>:
    a. People and their ways of accomplishing their respective tasks
    b. Attitudes
    c. Perspectives on job responsibilities
    d. Work ethic
    e. Character
    f. Desires for fulfillment
    g. Ways of improvement to build the person and the production
    h. Defining a win
    i. Knowing what a person's job does for him or her
    j. Allocating personnel resources better: what are the ways?
    k. Use of volunteers if applicable: acquisition, training, motivation, celebration

2. Materiel:
   a. Tools our people use to accomplish their tasks: work space, environment, equipment
   b. Needs for training to maximize tool use
   c. Allocation of appropriate tools for appropriate tasks
   d. Identifying needs for additional tools
   e. Keeping informed about changes in technology, acquiring better tools, and appropriate applications of new tools that are acquired

3. Time: the opportunities for accomplishment of required and donated tasks
   a. Time management: use of "on the job" time—prioritization
   b. Follow-through on projects
   c. Communication effectiveness, honoring the "other person's" time and closing communication loops
   d. Use of volunteer's time
   e. Multi-tasking
   f. Productivity

The RNA is conducted in confidential, individual appointments. Questions concerning three primary categories of resources will be presented to core team members. The questions are presented below. In these sessions we ask for complete honesty in dialogue and answers. Only in a context of heightened trust and truth can we secure the clearest picture possible to help us achieve and contribute more and become the best possible stewards of our resources.

Questions:

Category: Personnel

1. What are your positional responsibilities?
2. What does your job do for you?
3. What is a win (success) for you?
4. Are we using you, your abilities, talents and gifts resourcefully?
5. How can we utilize your abilities, talents and gifts better?
6. Please describe your work ethic.
7. How well do you handle "extra tasks" above and beyond the normal requirements of your job?
8. How do you deal with conflict?
9. How do you solve problems?
10. On a scale of 1 – 10, 10 the most successful, rate your effectiveness in accomplishing your designated tasks.

Category: Materiel

1. What are your current and available materiel resources?
2. Which of these do you use most often?
3. Which of these do you use seldom, if at all?
4. Are there any tools you have which you don't use, which you do not need?
5. Please evaluate your stewardship of the tools you use.
6. What additional resources do you think you need to accomplish your job better?
7. Please give examples of use of your materiel resources where you see efficiency achieved at least 90% of the time.
8. What kinds of training on the tools you use now would make you more productive?
9. How current do you think we are in acquisition and implementation of new tools?
10. Are you aware of new tools that if acquired would cause overall production to rise?

Category: Time

1. What is the total of your working hours per week?
2. How many hours of overtime do you work per week (if applicable)?
3. Are you satisfied with your schedule?
4. Can you describe how you best use your time?
5. Are assignments by you completed ahead of time, on time, or behind time? Please give percentages to equal 100%.
6. Are you organized well? Please describe how you organize your tasks.
7. How does your organization of your responsibilities make you more time-efficient?
8. When you are working against a deadline, how do you re-allocate your time to accomplish extra tasks?
9. How much time do you waste?
10. Do you multi-task? If so, how efficient are you, and do you find multi-tasking fulfilling?

Considerations:

The challenges of completing this Resource Needs Assessment:

1. Looking behind and learning from the past, and dedicating yourself unreservedly to becoming all you can become as a productive core team member

2. Being open to new methods where they can be shown to be true methods that best allocate resources and generate positive and productive results
3. Applying what we are learning so that learning becomes living
4. Planning proactively for future achievement in a goal-directed and verifiable time line

The <u>choices</u> of seeing new opportunities for growth, and changing from within:

1. Correcting poor choices (strengthening weaker areas)
2. Obedience and submission to agreed core values: the keys to humbling ourselves
3. Committing to living in right choices coming from agreement to the core values

The <u>consequences</u> of choosing well and applying your choices in daily life and work:

1. Better allocation of existing and future resources: personnel, materiel, and time
2. Heightened stewardship to know you are returning investments with interest
3. Celebrating the results across the board

Thank you for your participation in the Resource Needs Assessment. Your contributions will benefit the organization greatly as together we seek to allocate existing and future resources more effectively as individuals, and as members of the core teams we represent.

Creative
Team
Resources
Group

Personnel Review and Planning Document

Page 1 of 2

Employee Name and Identification: _____

Department or Core Team: _____

Date of Review: _____ Supervisor: _____

Instructions: Please complete the answers to the questions below in writing, and submit to your supervisor no later than three working days prior to your Review. Thank you.

1. How fulfilling is your work with our company?
2. What would you like to see changed to make your experience at our company better?
3. In what areas do you need to improve?
4. In what areas would you like training?
5. What additional tools do you need to accomplish your job well?
6. What are your gratifying accomplishments within this last period?
7. What can your supervisor do to help your work experience become more beneficial to you?
8. How involved do you wish to be in solution discussions for the problems the organization may face?
9. What are your greatest strengths?
10. What are your most significant weaknesses?

11. What do you bring to the table in terms of desire or capability that we haven't seen yet?
12. What brings you the most joy in your work for this organization?
13. What are the sources of your greatest stress points in your work?
14. What should the differences be in your core team's communication styles and techniques, internally and externally?
15. How do you view our vendors?
16. How do you view our customers?
17. How do you view others on your core team?
18. What is the environment you most prefer in which to accomplish your tasks?
19. What do you do to contribute to the environment you desire?
20. To what behavioral changes are you going to commit during this next period?
21. How will you know you have achieved the successes you desire?

Thank you for completing the answers to the questions above. We look forward to discussing these with you.

Position Account and Contribution Evaluation (PACE)

Sample Form **

> ** This form is subject to alteration and is designed to be a sample template from which an organization creates its own evaluation form. Check with your HR professional for compliance with applicable law and necessary rules and requirements, including important information for the design and use of any form your company employs.

Date of Completion of this PACE: _____

Page 1 of 5

Employee Information:

Employee Name	Position/Title	Identification #	Department	Supervisor

Date of Hire	Date of Review	Date Next Review	Review Type	Score System

Overall Score: _____

An action plan is required if the employee receives a work performance score of less than acceptable, beneath 'average,' or it is clearly shown that a fundamental imbalance exists between relationship and function from an overall point of view.

Position Summary and Purpose:

    A.
    B.
    C.
    D.

Position Qualification and Requirements:

    A.
    B.
    C.
    D.

Effectiveness Determiners:

    A. Required Education, Courses, Training
        1.
        2.
        3.
    B. Additional Requirements
        1.
        2.
        3.

Required Certification/Registration(s):
- A.
- B.
- C.

Position Evaluation Factors:
- A.
- B.
- C.

Supervision Given or Required:
- A.
- B.
- C.

Position Account and Contribution Evaluation (PACE) Standards

This account of your position and the evaluation of your contributions within it include two aspects of your performance: the decisions you make (relationships) and what you do (functions) that are associated and required with your job. These descriptions are not designed to be exhaustive and, with your full knowledge and at the discretion of your employer, may be modified from time to time, temporarily or permanently. Both employer and employee expect that additional tasks may be considered to be "non-essential," "supplementary," or "auxiliary" to the primary focus points of your position. Employer and employee concur that these needs will be met within reasonable expectations and cooperation, based on full agreement. Employer and employee value contributions in primary and additional areas. Employer and employee see these to be parts of essential efforts in achieving balance in relationship and function.

Relational Behaviors: The following behaviors contribute to the organization and division's Values, Vision, Mission and Message.

1. Behaviors supporting quality and contribution improvement efforts:

Unacceptable	Need Improvement	Acceptable	Superior

- Observation:

- Action Plan:

- Follow-Up Meeting:

2. Behaviors demonstrating appropriate application of resources:

   Unacceptable   Need Improvement   Acceptable   Superior

   - Observation:
   - Action Plan:
   - Follow-Up Meeting:

3. Office/Workplace Interaction (professional commitment, care, and communication):

   Unacceptable   Need Improvement   Acceptable   Superior

   - Observation:
   - Action Plan:
   - Follow-Up Meeting:

4. Behaviors contributing to Core Team goals:

   Unacceptable   Need Improvement   Acceptable   Superior

   - Observation:
   - Action Plan:
   - Follow-Up Meeting:

5. Behaviors demonstrating dependability, faithfulness and high accountability:

   Unacceptable   Need Improvement   Acceptable   Superior

   - Observation:
   - Action Plan:
   - Follow-Up Meeting:

Functional Behaviors: The following behaviors contribute to the organization and division's Values, Vision, Mission and Message.

This position and pay rate is expected to be performed at level [choose one]:

_____ Beginning
_____ Intermediate
_____ Advanced

If competencies of the essential functions are not consistently met at the agreed level of designation, a change in pay rate, corrective action, or release from [Company Name] may result.

1. Completion of overall tasks:

Unacceptable   Beginning   Intermediate   Advanced

- Observation:

- Action Plan:

- Follow-Up Meeting:

2. Concise and clear communication and follow-through:

Unacceptable   Beginning   Intermediate   Advanced

- Observation:

- Action Plan:

- Follow-Up Meeting:

3. Supplemental and auxiliary duties:

Unacceptable   Beginning   Intermediate   Advanced

- Observation:

- Action Plan:

- Follow-Up Meeting:

4. Contributions exceeding basic requirements:

      Unacceptable   Beginning   Intermediate   Advanced

- Observation:

- Action Plan:

- Follow-Up Meeting:

General Comments from Evaluator and Employee:

Evaluator:

Employee:

Signatures

My signature indicates that the contents of this PACE document were discussed with me and I was given the opportunity to make written comments. My signature does not necessarily imply that I agree with this PACE evaluation.

Employee _____ Date _____

Evaluator _____ Date _____

In attendance at this PACE Interview:

Supervisor _____   Other _____

    Other _____   Other _____

Final Thoughts and Reinforcement

Industrial Strength Solutions places the responsibility of needful change squarely in the arena of the person who desires the change. So much of the activity of building a business life investment model, one that works now and endures beyond its creator, is dependent solely on the character of the person who wants to "make it better" through the model he or she provides — and becomes the catalyst of positive change in his or her work environment.

Listed here are some of the actions in the business life investment model you may wish to take to assure a great mix and an enduring solution. Your model begins, is sustained, and develops if you decide to be the person who:

1. Enters a process of change eagerly, based on profound desires for something better.
2. Examines his or her constitution and motives, first.
3. Embarks on a process of improvement through behavioral changes, working to become the best he or she can be.
4. Eradicates negative attitudes that could destroy meaning and momentum of a worthwhile venture.
5. Eliminates unnecessary baggage from the journey of development, learning from the past and planning for the future.

6. Engages in pro-active processes of work ethics coming from a solid work ethic, willfully and with enthusiasm.
7. Embraces others, welcoming diversity of experience and environment while unreservedly committing to upholding shared core team values.
8. Entrusts confidence into like-minded individuals on a core team who share essential values and desires for winning.
9. Encourages others on the core team by taking time to communicate and contribute to their successes.
10. Empowers others on the team by participating in agreed agendas, cooperating fully to achieve the group's goals.
11. Emulates others who have shown in their attitudes and actions how principles in practice work over time, proven through test.
12. Establishes actions based on principle and wholeheartedly contributes to the success of teammates.
13. Enfolds the solid character traits upon which the core team is agreed and from which its contributions stem, into the consistent output of the workplace.
14. Expresses sincere appreciation and gratefully receives it.
15. Entertains new ideas, originating and promoting creativity.
16. Encounters problems with a solution mind-set and verifiable action.
17. Erases and replaces consuming negative attitudes, such as bitterness and blame, through applying positive solution provision.
18. Expands horizons of hope and optimism based on the successes of the team.
19. Evaluates success or failure objectively and begins correction from within.
20. Enhances the growth of the core team's members by personally building a duplicating and enduring model of faithfulness.

21. Echoes and accurately reflects the agreements from the core team to others who observe and may wish to become part of the action or replicate the model.
22. Experiences the deliverables of people and production, promotes balance on the team, and celebrates the results.

An *Industrial Strength Solutions* participant builds a durable business life investment model when these actions are employed. The question posed at the beginning of the book should be re-stated at the end. "Will you engage and become an ingredient in the creation of success mixtures on your team?" Let's see.

Creative
Team
Resources
Group

www.ctrg.com * www.LeadershipIs.com

www.Industrial-Strength-Solutions.com

CTRG provides quality resources for the development of teams within organizations whose desires are to grow and develop their personnel and achieve greater results in product or service provision. CTRG gives people great information that allows them to make changes in how they live and work and does this through building core teams. Our resources include personnel training, seminars, counsel, one-on-one and small-group leadership coaching, books, and instruction manuals.

Our foundational principle is that people are more important than production and relationships precede and give definition to function. The value of a person's contributions comes from that person's inherent worth. The value of the person causes the contributions a person makes to achieve even greater results.

Contact CTRG at the websites above. We will demonstrate first-hand how our team building principles can work for you. Glen Aubrey, President and CEO, along with other CTRG staff are available to your group for speaking engagements, on-site training and leadership coaching. CTRG looks forward to serving and working with you!

Acknowledgments

In the composition and completion phases of creating a book, the list of people to whom to express heartfelt appreciation grows as the networks expand and the older and established relationships blend with those of newer vintage. My family plays the key roles of support and encouragement, and for these contributions I sincerely thank my wife, Cindy, daughter Heather and her husband Neil, our son, Justin, who created the initial design for the book's cover (please see a collection of his original artwork at www.shadesofyou.net), and my mother, Zela. And for providing unlimited hours of enduring loyalty and love I want to acknowledge our little dog, Sadie. Yes, she owns us. A treat will follow.

The very gifted and dedicated people who make Creative Team Resources Group, Inc. work continue to inspire me as they provide essential help in the day-to-day activities of the business, as well as thoughtful, thorough and challenging points of view as the book's processes unfolded. These folks are not only working partners, these are great friends: Jeff Goble, Jordan Peck, Mark Chrysler, Steve Duff, Lynn Smith, Keith Koellish, and Janelle Luz.

Many other family members, friends, clients and business associates could be listed as providers and encouragers, whose contacts and associations down through the years have deeply enhanced our friendships and added greater meaning to our lives. Creating that list is a task that would prove, at once upon its completion, an outdated enterprise, simply because people and brand new relationships are being added to our growth constantly. It shouldn't be any other way. So let's sum up the acknowledgments with this: a final thank you to those client friends and new acquaintances who allowed their names and stories to be included in *Industrial Strength Solutions*: Rick and Patti Fleming and Tonya Weddington, Tom Clark, Richard Willis, Kathy Armstrong, Mary Ann Compher, Larry McNamer, Jo Ann Suarez, Doug Gadker, and John Gibson. Your contributions hit home. I am grateful to you.

I wish to thank President and Mrs. George W. Bush for the encounter at St. John's Church and the lessons I learned through it, Tyler Deyling for arranging it, and Marguerite A. Murer, Special Assistant to the President and Director of Presidential Correspondence, for her communication with me regarding telling the story in the book.

At PublishAmerica we were privileged to work with Ashley Patterson, Jeannette Gartrell, Jennifer Blaszka, and Dustin Putman.

All in all it can be seen that the soluble mixtures of dedicated efforts like those utilized in the creation of *Industrial Strength Solutions* produce a good example of workable solutions, the evidence of a core team in action, a group of dedicated, faithful people who are committed to principle, practice, perseverance, and production. All of them are more important than what they do, and what they have done is very important. It has been my honor to participate with them in the creation of this book.